Druids: A Very Short Introduction

VERY SHORT INTRODUCTIONS are for anyone wanting a stimulating and accessible way into a new subject. They are written by experts, and have been translated into more than 45 different languages.

The series began in 1995, and now covers a wide variety of topics in every discipline. The VSI library now contains over 500 volumes—a Very Short Introduction to everything from Psychology and Philosophy of Science to American History and Relativity—and continues to grow in every subject area.

Titles in the series include the following:

AFRICAN HISTORY John Parker and
  Richard Rathbone
AGEING Nancy A. Pachana
ALGEBRA Peter M. Higgins
AMERICAN HISTORY Paul S. Boyer
AMERICAN IMMIGRATION
  David A. Gerber
AMERICAN LEGAL HISTORY
  G. Edward White
AMERICAN POLITICAL HISTORY
  Donald Critchlow
AMERICAN POLITICAL PARTIES
  AND ELECTIONS L. Sandy Maisel
AMERICAN POLITICS
  Richard M. Valelly
THE AMERICAN PRESIDENCY
  Charles O. Jones
AMERICAN SLAVERY
  Heather Andrea Williams
ANARCHISM Colin Ward
ANCIENT EGYPT Ian Shaw
ANCIENT GREECE Paul Cartledge
THE ANCIENT NEAR EAST
  Amanda H. Podany
ANCIENT PHILOSOPHY Julia Annas
ANCIENT WARFARE Harry Sidebottom
ANGLICANISM Mark Chapman
THE ANGLO-SAXON AGE John Blair
ANIMAL BEHAVIOUR
  Tristram D. Wyatt
ANIMAL RIGHTS David DeGrazia
ANXIETY Daniel Freeman and
  Jason Freeman
ARCHAEOLOGY Paul Bahn

ARISTOTLE Jonathan Barnes
ART HISTORY Dana Arnold
ART THEORY Cynthia Freeland
ASTROPHYSICS James Binney
ATHEISM Julian Baggini
THE ATMOSPHERE Paul I. Palmer
AUGUSTINE Henry Chadwick
BACTERIA Sebastian G. B. Amyes
BARTHES Jonathan Culler
BEAUTY Roger Scruton
THE BIBLE John Riches
BLACK HOLES Katherine Blundell
BLOOD Chris Cooper
THE BRAIN Michael O'Shea
THE BRICS Andrew F. Cooper
BRITISH POLITICS Anthony Wright
BUDDHA Michael Carrithers
BUDDHISM Damien Keown
BUDDHIST ETHICS Damien Keown
BYZANTIUM Peter Sarris
CANCER Nicholas James
CAPITALISM James Fulcher
CATHOLICISM Gerald O'Collins
THE CELTS Barry Cunliffe
CHEMISTRY Peter Atkins
CHOICE THEORY Michael Allingham
CHRISTIANITY Linda Woodhead
CIRCADIAN RHYTHMS Russell Foster
  and Leon Kreitzman
CITIZENSHIP Richard Bellamy
CLASSICAL MYTHOLOGY
  Helen Morales
CLASSICS Mary Beard and
  John Henderson

Barry Cunliffe

DRUIDS

A Very Short Introduction

OXFORD
UNIVERSITY PRESS

OXFORD

UNIVERSITY PRESS

Great Clarendon Street, Oxford ox2 6DP

Oxford University Press is a department of the University of Oxford.
It furthers the University's objective of excellence in research, scholarship,
and education by publishing worldwide in

Oxford New York

Auckland Cape Town Dar es Salaam Hong Kong Karachi
Kuala Lumpur Madrid Melbourne Mexico City Nairobi
New Delhi Shanghai Taipei Toronto

With offices in

Argentina Austria Brazil Chile Czech Republic France Greece
Guatemala Hungary Italy Japan Poland Portugal Singapore
South Korea Switzerland Thailand Turkey Ukraine Vietnam

Oxford is a registered trade mark of Oxford University Press
in the UK and in certain other countries

Published in the United States
by Oxford University Press Inc., New York

British Library Cataloguing in Publication Data

Data available

Library of Congress Cataloging in Publication Data

Data available

Typeset by SPI Publisher Services, Pondicherry, India
Printed and bound by
CPI Group (UK) Ltd, Croydon, CR0 4YY

ISBN 978-0-19-953940-6

Contents

Preface

The Druids have been a subject of fascination since first they were encountered by Classical writers perhaps as early as the 4th century BC. The Renaissance brought those Classical descriptions to the attention of scholars, and in doing so unleashed a flood of books devoted to druidism – a flood that shows no sign of abating and to which this present essay is a small contribution.

Each generation interprets the Druids according to their own perspectives and prejudices, and therein lies one of the fascinations of the subject. What I have attempted to do here is quite simple. First, I distinguish the literary evidence from the detail of archaeology and present them separately to prevent the comfortable circularity of argument that has sometimes intruded upon the discussion, and secondly I have tried to deconstruct the narratives so that each set of sources can be seen in the contexts in which they were written. In this way, I hope, it will be possible to understand the dynamics of the subject. Over the 800 years or so from c. 400 BC to AD 400, the Druid caste changed dramatically, as did the society of which they were a part. The last 500 years has seen our vision of them change equally as rapidly. The fascination of the subject lies in teasing out these threads in an attempt to understand the transforming power of time.

List of illustrations

Chapter 1
The Druids in time and space

Every midsummer solstice hundreds of 'Druids' flock to Stonehenge in the middle of Salisbury Plain to celebrate the midsummer sunrise. For them, and indeed for the many others who visit just to enjoy the occasion, it is a moment to feel the timelessness of being – it gives the reassurance of stability in a frightening, ever-changing world and the sense of being part of a community whose roots go deep into prehistory. It is a place to contemplate the profound rhythms of time. Perhaps it has always been thus.

More recently, those who regard themselves to be Druids have extended their claim to the past. One group has stated its belief that the bones of a young woman, buried near Avebury some 4,000 years ago, are those of a tribal ancestor and has demanded that they should be returned to them for burial. Even the more moderate Council of British Druid Orders (COBDO) states that: 'It is the policy of the Council of British Druid Orders that the sacred remains of our brothers and sisters should be returned to the living landscape from which they were taken.'

To most archaeologists and scientists this is a nonsense. The debris of the past, be it flint tools, potsherds, or human skeletons, is valuable, indeed unique, evidence that can be made to tell a story of our prehistory and should be curated for future generations to continue to study using new techniques as they become available. Many would argue that the modern Druids are a complete reinvention with no legitimacy – a confection dreamed up by fertile imaginations to gratify personal needs. At best, they are an eccentricity to be tolerated; at worst, a threat to rationality to be challenged.

The Druids have been written and talked about probably since well before 300 BC. Each generation has taken a view and through the vagaries of time scraps of these opinions have come down to us, allowing the fascination of picking through the morass of observations, polemics, distortions, and wishful thinkings, in the hope of arriving at a narrative of druidism as objective as the data will allow. The texts mentioning Druids are drawn from wide tracts of territory over long spans of time. To stitch together a mention in a Classical Greek source with a Welsh Tudor document in order to create a vision of 'the Druid' is an obvious nonsense – discontinuity and change caused by time and space must be taken into account.

Standing back from the detail – with which we will engage later – the documentary evidence available to us can be divided into three broad clusters. First, there are the observations made by Greeks and Romans, and selectively repeated in later texts. The earliest of these may date to the 4th century BC, the latest to the 7th century AD. What survives is only a tiny fragment of what must originally have been written. Then we have the vivid tales and myths of the Irish and Welsh vernacular literature – essentially a deeply rooted oral tradition that was eventually committed to written text between the 8th and 11th centuries AD by Christian clerics. Oral traditions change over time with the telling, and Christian scribes were not averse to editing and interpolation. Finally, after a period of silence, comes the rediscovery of the past as Classical texts are identified in monastic libraries and published, and the search begins for national origins. By the 17th century, Druids are frequently mentioned, and in the 18th century the notion of the ancient priesthood, intermixed with myths about the Celts, is avidly romanticized as the process of reinvention gets under way. Since our concern in this book is with the real Druids, we will necessarily concentrate on the Classical and vernacular sources. The reinvented Druids, created Frankenstein-like from a few scraps of real data and a great deal of imagination, fascinating though they are as a phenomenon reflecting human needs and susceptibilities, will be touched on rather more briefly in the concluding chapters.

So who were the Druids? The Classical texts ascribe to them a formidable variety of functions: they were philosophers, teachers, judges, the repository of communal wisdoms about the natural world and the traditions of the people, and the mediators between humans and the gods. According to Julius Caesar, 'The Druids are in charge of religion. They have control over public and private sacrifices and give rulings on all religious questions' (*BG* VI.13). Yet, curiously, they are never referred to directly as priests (*sacerdos*). In later texts and the vernacular literature, they appear more as mystics and magicians. Given the range of attributes, it is probably best to regard them as a caste of intellectuals. Caesar's famous generalization, that in Gaul there are only two classes of men who are of any account or importance – the Druids and the Knights – puts them on a par with the tribal elite.

The territorial extent of druidism is not easy to define. The Classical texts tell of Druids only in Gaul (France) and in Britain, while the vernacular sources make it clear that Druids were also to be found in Ireland. Strictly, then, druidism is to be seen as a phenomenon restricted to the northern part of Atlantic Europe. However, the absence of reference to Druids in other parts of Europe does not necessarily imply that they were not more widespread. Indeed, some writers have assumed that Druids were coterminous with the Celts of the La Tène period (after c. 450 BC) and that the caste spread with the migration of Celtic communities into the Po valley, the Carpathian Basin, Transylvania, and along the Danube into the Balkans, and eventually, in the 3rd century, into Anatolia. In support of this is often quoted the place-name *Drunemeton* where the Council of the Galatians met in central Anatolia. The name may roughly be translated as the 'sanctuary in the oak grove' and belongs to the group of *'nemeton'* place-names found across the Celtic world signifying a sacred place. While this *could* allow that Druids served the Celtic immigrants in Anatolia, it does not imply that they did. There is no need to suppose that this highly specialist caste of wise men (assuming they were in existence at this time) chose to migrate with the mobile factions of the community who moved out of their western European homeland in the 5th century. A sacred place suggests the presence of priests but not necessarily Druids.

If, then, we take the cautious view in locating the Druids in Gaul, Britain, and Ireland, the question arises where and when did druidism arise? Julius Caesar is quite explicit:

> It is thought that the doctrine of the Druids was invented in Britain and was brought from there to Gaul; even today those who want to study the doctrine in greater detail usually go to Britain to learn there.

(*BG* VI.13)

Since there was no particular propaganda value in this statement, we may accept that Caesar was directly quoting either what he had been told by Gaulish informants or had read in a source no longer extant. How valid this belief was it is impossible to say but there is no reason why it should not have been true. We will return to this matter again below, in Chapter 2. On the question of when druidism emerged, there is little that can safely be said. There are reasons to suggest that Druids existed in the 4th century BC (see Chapter 4) and it could be argued, as we shall endeavour to do later, that the caste has its roots deep in prehistory, possibly as far back as the 2nd millennium. There is no reason at all to assume that druidism was solely a feature of the La Tène Iron Age.

4

How, then, do we know about the Druids? The earliest sources are Classical writers living in the Mediterranean region who chose to write about the barbarian peoples of western Europe. Principal among them are Julius Caesar (100–44 BC), Diodorus Siculus (late 1st century BC to early 1st century AD), Strabo (c. 63 BC to AD 21+), Pliny the Elder (AD 23–79), Tacitus (AD 55–120), Athenaeus (fl. c. AD 200), and a number of Greeks who, in the first few centuries AD, were compiling encyclopaedic works using an array of texts available to them in the libraries of Alexandria. The intriguing problem is that, with the partial exception of Julius Caesar, all were using second-hand sources whose authors had probably never encountered the Druids for themselves. Their quotations are partial, selected, and are coloured to suit the viewpoint of the author and the prejudices of the time. Thus they need careful handling. It is necessary to identify the original sources and to assess the processes of transmission. We must also try to understand how druidism changed over time and how the Classical perception of the Druids changed. We are dealing with highly dynamic processes of change, the only clues to which are the surviving words of a few Greek and Roman writers.

It is quite conceivable that the number of original sources – that is, people who actually observed Druids – was very small. Julius Caesar is certainly one. He was present in Gaul subduing its inhabitants from 58 to 51 BC and made two brief expeditions to Britain in 55 and 54 BC. During this time, he had ample opportunity to observe the Gauls and Britons and, while he may have had access to earlier accounts, it is likely that his famous account of the Druids in his war commentaries, *De Bello Gallico* VI.13, was based, in some part at least, on his actual first-hand experiences. One of the Gauls he befriended, Divitiacus, was himself a Druid.

Two broadly contemporary writers, Strabo and Diodorus, together with the 2nd-century AD writer Athenaeus, used an earlier text that is generally agreed to be the lost works of Posidonius (c. 135–

c. 50 BC), a Stoic philosopher born in Apamea in Syria. Posidonius travelled widely in the western Mediterranean including coastal Gaul to collect information first hand for his great work *Histories*, published in the early 1st century BC. *Histories* no longer survives in its original form but was widely quoted and seems to have been the major source from which Diodorus Siculus and Strabo obtained their information on the Celts and the Druids. Athenaeus also used the work, and some have argued that Caesar may have augmented his first-hand knowledge with details derived from Posidonius.

The communities with whom Posidonius would have come into contact in his travels in southern Gaul in the early decades of the 1st century BC had been exposed to the influence of the many Greek cities which developed around the shores of the Golfe du Lion following the foundation of the first colony of Massalia (Marseilles) around 600 BC. They had also experienced the movement of the Roman armies, marching to and fro across their territory to the wars in Iberia throughout much of the 2nd century BC. Finally, in 123 BC, the Roman armies moved in to take possession of the whole coastal region and the lower valley of the Rhône, creating what was to become the Roman province of Gallia Transalpina. Unless Posidonius had managed to penetrate far inland, the Gauls he encountered are those most likely to have been influenced by their long exposure to Mediterranean culture. Posidonius, clearly an acute observer, was well aware that he was seeing a people in a state of transformation. This sense of change is made explicit when in one description of Celtic behaviour (quoted by Strabo) he uses the phrase 'and in former times' to preface his account.

The Posidonian tradition was clearly influential in late 1st-century BC accounts of Celts and Druids, but once the Roman armies had taken control of Gaul during Caesar's campaigns in the 50s, and 90 years later had spread through much of Britain following the Claudian invasion of AD 43, many Romans – soldiers,

Druids

administrators, and traders – would have had the opportunity to have come face to face with Druids, should they have so chosen. We have already suggested that Caesar's account of Druids is likely to have been largely based on his first-hand experiences, and we know that one Gaulish Druid, Divitiacus, visited Rome and had conversations with Cicero. A century later, the Roman armies fighting their way across Britain faced resistance led by Druids. These encounters fed in new knowledge which may have informed the descriptions of 1st- and 2nd-century AD writers like Lucan (AD 39–65), Pomponius Mela (fl. c. AD 43), Tacitus (AD 55–120), and Suetonius (early 2nd century AD). But in the new Imperial age, there was a new imperative – to depict the Druids as the leaders of a vicious sect that revelled in human sacrifice – thus providing a moral justification for conquest. While, in the Posidonian tradition, the Celts and Druids were presented in the comforting, if patronizing, guise of 'the noble savage', under the Imperial tradition they had become the enemy who must be destroyed in the name of humanity. The demonization of others to justify aggression is a familiar political ploy.

The travels of Posidonius and the *Histories* he wrote undoubtedly contributed considerably to knowledge of the Druids, but in the surviving Classical literature, particularly the writings of the Alexandrian encyclopaedists, there is evidence that earlier sources were available in the libraries of Alexandria. The process of transmission is open to debate (and we will explore this later), but it is widely believed that among the earliest sources to be used were the works of Timaeus (c. 356–c. 270 BC), a Greek historian and ethnographer who lived at Tauromenium in Sicily and wrote extensively on Sicilian history and the west Mediterranean.

The writings of Timaeus are known to us only through quotations surviving in the works of others. Not only was he a primary source on the Druids for the later Alexandrian historians, but he was also quoted widely by Diodorus Siculus and Pliny the Elder on matters of Atlantic geography. Where, then, did this Sicilian, who spent the last 50 years of his life in exile in Athens, learn of Gaul, the Atlantic, and the North Sea? The most likely answer is from a book, *On the Ocean*, written by his near-contemporary, Pytheas of Massalia, about 320 BC. Pytheas travelled widely along the Atlantic coasts of Gaul, circumnavigated Britain, and was the first to write about these distant regions. It was probably largely through the works of Timaeus and the astronomer and geographer Dikaiarkhos of Messene that the writings of Pytheas became known to later authors in the Mediterranean: both quote him as a primary source.

While it is tempting to expand upon the intriguing paths by which knowledge of the European barbarians was transmitted in the Classical world, we must restrict ourselves to what is relevant to the Druids. To summarize: Pytheas wrote extensively on the peoples of north-western Gaul and Britain whom he knew from first-hand observation, and his book was used as a primary source by Timaeus, who was himself quoted as the source of information on the Druids by the later Alexandrian writers. It is not unreasonable therefore to suggest that Pytheas may have been the ultimate origin of the Alexandrian tradition. But Pytheas was also the source of information on the Atlantic regions used by Diodorus Siculus and Pliny the Elder. Could it be that these writers also derived their information about the Druids directly from him? Pliny's famous description of white-robed Druids cutting mistletoe with a golden sickle (see below) is so unlike the Posidonian and Imperial traditions that it could well have come from something much earlier. It is even possible that Posidonius, and after him Strabo and Diodorus Siculus, derived some of his information on the Druids directly from Pytheas to augment his own observations. These issues are entertaining to debate but are unlikely ever to be resolved with any degree of certainty.

Leaving aside the detail, we may conclude that the corpus of knowledge on the Druids available to the Classical world derived from first-hand observations made by Greek travellers like

Pytheas (c. 325 BC) and Posidonius (c. 125 BC), and by Roman generals like Caesar (c. 50 BC) and those who followed him – soldiers and administrators – into the barbarian regions of north-western Europe. What they learned was selected and nuanced to suit the mood of the time and the political imperatives that prevailed. Clearly, this is material which needs to be handled with great care.

The vernacular literature of Ireland and Wales provides a totally different set of sources complete with their own problems of interpretation. The position with regard to the Irish literature is succinctly summed up by Barry Raftery:

> … the Irish sources present us with an immense body of material combining fact and fantasy, myth and legend, ancient lore, Classical interpolation, pan-Christian fables and medieval folk tradition. As a source of information on the Irish Iron Age it provides us with a challenge of exceptional complexity.
>
> (*Pagan Celtic Ireland*, p. 13)

This is not the place to engage with the challenge, but something must be said of the nature of the surviving texts in relation to the information they provide on the existence and practices of the Druids.

There are two broad categories of texts – the sagas and the Law tracts. The sagas can be divided into four cycles of tales: the Mythological Cycle, the Ulster Cycle, the Fenian Cycle, and the Historical Cycle. Of these, the Ulster Cycle is the oldest of the early Irish sources: it consists of about 80 separate stories, the most famous being the *Táin Bó Cuailnge* ('The Cattle Raid of Cooley'); the others are much shorter and are ancillary, though linked, to the theme and characters of the *Táin*. There are several manuscripts which contain versions of all or part of the *Táin*. The earliest of these (Recension I) is preserved in a manuscript known as *The Book of the Dun Cow* which was composed in the monastery of Clonmacnoise at the end of the 11th century. A fuller version (Recension II), incorporating additional material but omitting interpolations and duplications, is given in the *Book of Leinster*, dating to the end of the 12th century, which may have been the product of the monastic establishment at Oughaval in Co. Laois. Recension I was composed from two earlier manuscripts, now lost, and there are reasons to believe that the tales may first have been written down as early as the 7th century. Before that the sagas were kept alive by oral transmission through the performances of storytellers. How deeply rooted in the past they were it is impossible to say for certain, but scholars are generally agreed that the sagas of the Ulster Cycle were being proclaimed at least as early as the early 5th century AD and are likely to be considerably older.

What survive for us to enjoy today, in the vigorous and colourful texts translated from the 11th- and 12th-century manuscripts, are the end products – the fossilization – of continuously changing stories, each retelling and, later, each rewriting creatively modifying what had gone before. The oral tales, proclaimed in heightened dramatic form to enthralled audiences in the 5th century, were no doubt very different in emphasis, structure, and detail to those written down by medieval Christian monks mindful to mould the stories to conform to the structure of Greek epic and the teachings of the scriptures and to include details of familiar material culture like Viking swords and silverwork.

Yet behind all the accretions and editings, there remains a saga rooted in the values and behaviour of pre-Roman Iron Age society familiar in the writings of Classical authors describing Gaulish and British society. It is a time of heroes, of Druids, of raiding, chariots, and head-hunting, and of great feasts at which the honour and status of individual warriors were proclaimed, contested, and affirmed in front of the assembled masses. It is tempting to think of this as a reflection of Iron Age Ireland – but is it? There are a number of inconsistencies, not least the evident importance of the chariot in the *Táin* and yet its total lack of visibility in the Irish archaeological record. The uncomfortable possibility remains that the stories around which the *Táin* was constructed were gleaned from a pan-European saga and made their own by Irish storytellers nostalgic for a distant heroic age. The Druids, as they appear in the Irish sagas, may, then, in part be memories of a caste modified by pagan Irish storytellers and emasculated by Christian monks. These issues are by no means settled, but it is as well to raise them lest we are drawn to use the Irish sagas too simplistically.

That said, there were Druids in early Ireland—they are attested in the *Lives* of the saints, in hymns, and in Law tracts codified in the 7th and 8th centuries—though by this time they are so reduced by Christianity as to be regarded as little more than magicians and witch doctors. The mood is captured by one 8th-century hymn that asks for God's protection from the spells of women, blacksmiths, and Druids! This is among the last contemporary references we have until the Druids of the Classical world begin to enter the consciousness of the late medieval age.

In the late Middle Ages, as the monastic libraries of Europe were being opened up to wider scholarship, the Classical texts which they had preserved for centuries came into the wider domain. With the advent of printing, they became further available in multiple copies to scholars throughout the Continent. Thus it was that Julius Caesar's *Commentaries on the Gallic War* burst on the world in a version printed in Venice in 1511, while Pliny's *Natural Histories* appeared in translation in 1601.

The French were the first to make use of the texts in the 16th century to bolster their quest for nationhood: a common Celtic ancestry became a powerful political tool at a time when Brittany was being incorporated into the French state. In England, the impact of the newly available Classical literature was delayed, and it was not until the end of the 16th century, when English translations of the Latin originals were becoming widely available, that Celts and Druids began to seep into the public consciousness. Speculation about our British ancestors was greatly stimulated by reports of 'savages' brought back from the New World by John White who, in 1585, had accompanied the group of Englishmen sent by Sir Walter Raleigh to found a colony on the coast of North Carolina. White's carefully observed drawings of Native Americans became the inspiration for Theodor de Bry's spirited images of ancient Britons published in 1590 – the first attempts to visualize prehistory.

It was during the 17th century that field archaeology began to develop in Britain with the travels of antiquarians through the countryside. The wonder of the great prehistoric monuments of Wessex – sites like Avebury and Stonehenge – soon made a firm impression on those who were trying to conceptualize prehistory, and inevitably debates about Druids and Stonehenge began to play a prominent part. While some writers like Inigo Jones, whose work was posthumously published in 1655, believed that the sophistication of Stonehenge meant that it had to be a Roman construction, others, like John Aubrey, believed it to be earlier. Writing in 1649 of Avebury and Stonehenge, he offered 'a humble submission to better judgements...that they were Temples of the Druids'. So it was that the long association in popular belief of Druids and Stonehenge grew out of the fertile minds of 17th-century antiquarians.

Many other writers warmed to the theme, most scanning the Classical texts for colourful detail they could weave into their constructed visions of the Druid priesthood. John Toland was an exception in that he also had a knowledge of the Irish vernacular literature which he used to good effect to fill out the picture. His views were finally published in *Critical History of the Celtic Religion* in 1740, later to be reissued under the more engaging title of *The History of the Druids*. It was in the same year that the antiquary William Stukeley published his famous

Stonehenge, a Temple Restored to the British Druids and three years later, *Abury, a Temple of the British Druids, with Some Others Described*. By the mid-18th century, then, the Druids had become firmly established in the consciousness of literate Britons. In this age of romanticism, they were presented as the wise priests of our noble savage ancestors, white-robed and bearded, practising their arts in sacred groves and in the many megalithic monuments scattered throughout the British countryside. This amusing confection has proved to be resilient and is still widely accepted in the more popular literature even today, 250 years after its creation.

In Brittany, too, enthusiasm for the Druids became infectious. In 1703, a Breton priest, Paul-Yves Pezron, published his *L'Antiquité de la Nation et la Langue des Celts* in which he put forward the view that the Gauls were descended from Celts who had migrated west from Anatolia and that the Bretons and the Welsh were their direct descendants. Pezron's theories were widely accepted, particularly in Brittany, not least because they offered an acceptable origins myth at a time when Breton culture was coming under pressure from the centralizing authorities in Paris. Megalithic tombs were soon ascribed to Druids, and in 1796 La Tour-d'Auvergne published his *Origines Gauloises celles plus anciens peuples de l'Europe* in which he introduced the word 'dolmen', based on the Breton *dolmin*, as a general term for megalithic tombs. By the turn of the century, *celtomania* had gripped the imagination, and in his *Monuments Celtiques* (1805), Jacques Cambry wrote enthusiastically of Breton megaliths and their deep Druidic and astronomical significance.

The antiquarians of the 17th and 18th centuries can be forgiven for their indulgences – they were groping in the dark, attempting to build a prehistory from the few scraps of data they had to hand – field monuments and artefacts devoid of a chronological framework and isolated references in the Classical sources. The narrative they created was of its age, and that Druids should feature so prominently is hardly surprising given the vividness with which they were treated by the ancient sources.

While many 18th-century scholars were striving for a truth, others were not afraid to invent. One of the most famous was a Welsh-born London stonemason, Edward Williams, or Iolo Morganwg as he preferred to be called. As an expatriate he became passionate about Welsh culture and tradition. But frustrated by the paucity of genuine sources, he began to fabricate what he felt ought to exist, claiming to have discovered early Welsh literary sources as well as traditions of lore and wisdom which, he said, linked directly back to the prehistoric Druids. Another of his colourful inventions was a Druidic ceremony which he called the Gorsedd. It was first enacted by expatriate Welshmen on Primrose Hill in London on the autumnal equinox of 1792 and used as props a ring of stones and a central stone altar on which lay an unsheathed sword. The extravagance could be excused as harmless nonsense and might have sunk into obscurity had it not been for the fact that in 1819 Iolo managed to have it added to the genuine ceremony of the *eisteddfod*, in that year held in Carmarthen. Thereafter it has remained part of the *eisteddfod*. Many observers today, unaware that the Gorsedd is entirely a figment of Iolo's opium-fuelled imagination, believe that the performing Druids are a genuine survival from the past.

Another 18th-century invention was a series of poems ascribed to Ossian, a semi-legendary Gaelic bard, and published by a Scot, James Macpherson, between 1760 and 1763. While Macpherson was well versed in Gaelic oral tradition and may even have had access to documents from the 16th century, it is evident that the 'Fragments of Ancient Poetry' which he published as genuine are largely fictitious. He longed that a great oral tradition had survived in Scotland and in its absence set about creating one.

The early 18th-century Romantics and the later 18th-century fabricators created a heady mix of fact, speculation, and sheer invention to fuel 19th-century enthusiasm for all things Celtic. The gentle, almost wistful, nostalgia of scholars like Ernest Renan, Matthew Arnold, and Lady Gregory for the tenuous and fast-disappearing Celtic heritage kept the subject very much alive, while archaeological discoveries began to add a new component – material culture – to the debate. The Druids could now be pictured holding aloft famous artefacts like the Battersea shield or the Waterloo Bridge helmet, as they offered prayers before consigning them to the gods of the River Thames!

From the time of the Romantics, there have been people who have believed themselves to be descendants of the ancient Druids and others who have been content to join in with invented ceremonies in the belief that they are taking part in rituals deeply rooted in time. Neodruidism is growing in popularity, as a glance at the internet will show. While of interest to those studying the sociology of belief, it must be stressed that neodruidism is a recently created phenomenon. Since it has no continuity with ancient druidism sketched for us by Classical writers, the two are best treated as totally separate subjects.

Chapter 2
The European theatre

There has been a tendency in the past to regard druidism as a largely western European phenomenon relating to the latter part of the Iron Age – the period archaeologists refer to as La Tène (named after artefacts deposited on the edge of Lake Neuchâtel in Switzerland). One of the reasons for this is that La Tène material culture is found in all the areas in which the Druids are attested by the Classical sources and it covers the period c. 450 BC to the Roman era – the period during which the same sources tell us the Druids were active. These coincidences do not, however, mean that druidism was restricted to this period: indeed, it is a reasonable assumption that the beliefs and practices that constitute druidism began earlier and were deeply rooted in western European prehistory. In this chapter we will examine some of these ritual practices in so far as they can be deduced from the scraps of archaeological evidence that survive.

Another assumption that needs to be addressed is that the Druids were the intellectual elite of the Celts. There is some truth in this. The Druids were active in Gaul in the 2nd and 1st centuries BC and, according to Julius Caesar, writing in the mid-1st century BC, the people living in the central part of Gaul between the Seine and the Garonne rivers called themselves Celts. An earlier observer, Pytheas, writing at the end of the 4th century BC, also describes the people living in the Atlantic part of this region as *Kelticē*. But how extensive were the Celts, and what were their origins and history, are currently the subjects of a lively and complex debate. The old, long-held view, that the Celts emerged in west-central Europe and spread from there eastwards to the Carpathian Basin and beyond as far as Anatolia, south into Italy and the Balkans, and west to Iberia, Britain, and Ireland, is only partly supported by the evidence. The eastward and southern movement has some validity in that the Classical sources document raids and migrations into these areas from the 4th to 2nd centuries BC, but there is no evidence, archaeological or textual, that supports the westerly movement. Yet the Greek and Roman texts speak of Celts in the west of Iberia in the 6th century and in Atlantic Gaul in the 4th, and there is growing evidence to suggest that the Celtic language was being spoken in the far south-west of Iberia as early as the 8th century.

How can all this be explained? If we accept that the prime characteristic of the Celt is speaking the Celtic language, the simplest view would be to suppose that the Celts emerged in Atlantic Europe in a zone stretching from the Algarve to Britain and Ireland, gaining a degree of cohesion from the fact that intense maritime activity bound the Atlantic-facing communities tightly together. In such a context, a common language would have evolved to facilitate communication and, as the river networks became increasingly used for systems of exchange, so the language was adopted by the more inland communities. By the 6th century, when our Classical sources begin, there were Celtic speakers in much of Iberia, Gaul, and probably Britain and Ireland. The famous Celtic migrations that began around 400 BC involved only people on the inland (eastern) periphery of the Celtic-speaking zone: it was they who moved to the south and east.

If this scenario is correct, how does it affect our understanding of the relationship between Celts and Druids? The simplest response would be to allow that druidism may have been a feature of Celtic culture. If so, it may have developed in the west of Europe and have spread to west-central Europe by the 5th century. In the period of migration that followed, it is possible that the beliefs and practices were carried by the migrating communities south into northern Italy and eastwards as far as Anatolia. The fact that there is no textual evidence of Druids in Iberia, northern Italy, or central and eastern Europe may simply be an accident of survival. In other words, we cannot say definitely that there were no Druids in these areas but simply that none are specifically mentioned in the surviving texts.

If this thesis of the westerly origins of the Celts is accepted, then druidism, like the development of the Celtic language, may have had its roots deep in the prehistory of Atlantic Europe. With this in mind, in the rest of this chapter we will review some of the evidence for religious beliefs and behaviour during the time from the beginning of the Neolithic period, in the middle of the 6th millennium, up to the middle of the 1st millennium, when the Classical sources begin to appear. Chapter 3 will look at the archaeological evidence for religious practice in the La Tène period when the historic Druids were known to have been active.

Tangible data reflecting behaviour conditioned by belief systems take a variety of forms in the archaeological record. Broadly speaking, it consists of burial rites, depositions, 'ritual' structures, and iconography – that is, the physical manifestations of behaviour as it impacts on the soil or is found in archaeological contexts. What we do not have access to are narratives of belief or the philosophy that underpins them. We may offer interpretations based on the physical evidence, but at best these interpretations will be incomplete and at worst biased by our preconceptions. That said, there is much to be learned from considering the evidence as dispassionately as possible.

Standing back from all the detail, a simple underlying pattern can be discerned which may be characterized as the balance of opposites between the earth and the sky – the fertile earth providing the sustenance essential for the community's wellbeing; the ever-consistent sky offering the signs that chart the passage of time. Both were inhabited by the gods, who had to be cajoled and placated. This stark oppositional model, variously interpreted by different prehistoric communities, offers a simple structure against which we can view and begin to understand the beliefs manifest in the scraps of archaeological evidence that survive.

The disposal of the dead has forever been a concern of human communities. Care for the dead body is evident in the Palaeolithic period, and by the Mesolithic period (9th to 5th millennia) cemeteries of carefully interred bodies are found along the maritime areas of western Europe, the individuals often being accompanied by items such as red deer antler, shell beads, and red ochre, which might be taken to imply some belief in the afterworld. Thereafter, 'grave goods', as they are called, frequently recur, with careful burials most notably in the 2nd millennium, when single interments were usually provided with sets of equipment which might reach elaborate proportions. The famous burial found in Bush Barrow, within sight of Stonehenge, was accompanied by bronze daggers and an axe, a sceptre, and gold ornaments, while his near contemporary, a female, buried at Upton Lovell, wore an amber necklace as well as various gold items. The temptation, when confronted with these arrays, is to think of the deceased being decked out in his or her finery and prepared for the afterlife – and so indeed it may have been – but the situation may well have been more complex.

To most societies, death is a process – a *rite de passage* – which begins with the last breath and ends when the spirit is at rest or has departed: the process may be very short or it may be extended. During this liminal period, the body may be treated in various ways. It may be placed on view as a visible assurance that the death has occurred and it may be the focus of offerings, relatives providing gifts to the corpse, thus demonstrating to others the strength and power of the lineage. In such a case, the objects buried with the dead may not necessarily be the personal equipment of the deceased but may instead reflect how his/her lineage wished to perceive themselves or wanted to be seen by others. In other words, grave goods may have other meanings than simply reflecting the life status of the deceased and a belief in the afterworld.

In some societies, the *rite de passage* may have been very extended, as is implied by evidence found in the megalithic tombs and earthen long barrows of the 4th and 3rd millennia. In the case of the earthen long barrows, the first stage of the ritual involved the construction of a timber mortuary enclosure in which bodies were laid out as they became available. This may have taken place over a considerable period until such time as the community decided to move to closure, which usually involved the digging of two parallel ditches and the piling up of the spoil over the mortuary enclosure to create a long mound. A similar process seems to have been implicit in the megalithic chambered tombs as, for example, in the West Kennet long barrow. Here it seems that the body of the newly deceased was placed in the main passage until such time that another person died, when the remains of the earlier body were cleared away into side chambers to make space for the new arrival. This went on for some time until the moment of closure, which here involved the placing of a massive stone slab across the entrance.

What beliefs lay behind these complex practices is difficult to say, but one possibility is that the long barrows and megalithic structures were tombs of elite lineages which were maintained in use until the last member of the group had died. The practice of single burial, which followed in the 2nd millennium, appears at first sight to be a major change in the belief system. However, it could be argued that the rows of barrows that dominate the chalk downs of southern Britain represent the burial grounds of single lineages, and that when the last of the lineage had died the cemetery simply ceased to grow.

Attempts to quantify death rates and burial numbers in 2nd-millennium Wessex have led to the conclusion that only a fraction of the population was given careful burial, the rest being disposed of in some other manner, most probably by excarnation, that is, the exposure of the body to the elements and to predatory birds. What social factors governed the selection we will never know, but the implications are interesting. One sector of the population was consigned to the earth – to the chthonic deities – the other to the sky. This same dichotomy, but expressed in a different way, is implicit in the rite of cremation, which begins to replace inhumation in the middle of the 2nd millennium. On the funeral pyre, the spirit of the departed is released into the sky while the physical remains, the ashes, are placed in ceramic containers and buried in the ground.

Although changes over time and regional differences complicate the picture, it is evident from the sketch given here that the belief systems involved in the disposal of the dead were sophisticated. In all probability, they encompassed a sense of a spirit that left the body during the *rite de passage* and a belief in the protective power of the chthonic and sky deities. Beyond this, however, it is difficult to venture.

The question of human sacrifice is worth considering. Though indisputable evidence is hard to find, excavation at the 3rd millennium causewayed camp of Hambledon Hill in Dorset showed that human skulls were placed at intervals in the ditches. This could be interpreted as evidence of sacrifice, but it could equally be that the skulls of ancestors were chosen to protect the hill from the intrusion of alien spirits. As so often with archaeological evidence, there are many possible explanations.

How far back in time European communities began to recognize and chart the movements of the sun, moon, and stars it is impossible to say, but for the mobile hunting bands of the Palaeolithic period, following large herds through the forests of

Europe and returning to base camps when the hunt was over, the ability to navigate using the stars would have been vital to existence. Similarly, indicators of the changing seasons would have signalled the time to begin specific tasks in the annual cycle of activity. For communities living by the sea, the tides provided a finer rhythm while tidal amplitude could be related to lunar cycles, offering a precise system for estimating the passage of time. The evening disappearance of the sun below the horizon must have been a source of wonder and speculation. Living close to nature, with one's very existence depending upon seasonal cycles of rebirth and death, inevitably focused the mind on the celestial bodies as indicators of the driving force of time. Once the inevitability of the seasonal cycles was fully recognized, it would have been a short step to believing that the movements of the sun and the moon had a controlling power over the natural world.

The spread of food-producing regimes into western Europe in the middle of the 6th millennium led to a more sedentary lifestyle and brought communities closer to the seasonal cycle, which governed the planting of crops and the management of flocks and herds. A proper adherence to the rhythm of time, and the propitiation of the deities who governed it, ensured fertility and productivity.

The sophistication of these early Neolithic communities in measuring time is vividly demonstrated by the alignments of the megalithic tombs and other monuments built in the 4th and 3rd millennia. The great passage tomb of New Grange in the Boyne Valley in Ireland was carefully aligned so that at dawn on the day of the midwinter solstice the rays of the rising sun would shine through a slot in the roof and along the passage to light up a triple spiral carved on an orthostat set at the back of the central chamber. The contemporary passage grave at Maes Howe on Orkney was equally carefully placed so that the light of the setting sun on the midwinter solstice would flow down the side of the passage before filling the central chamber at the end. The passage grave of Knowth, in the same group as New Grange, offers further refinements. Here there are two separate passages exactly aligned east to west: the west-facing passage captures the setting sun on the spring and autumn equinoxes (21 March and 21 September), while the east-facing passage is lit up by the rising sun on the same days. The nearby passage grave of Dowth appears to respect other solar alignments and, although it has not been properly tested, there is a strong possibility that the west-south-west orientation of its main passage was designed to capture the setting sun on the winter cross-quarter days (November and February) half way between the equinox and the solstice.

Other monuments, most notably stone circles, have also been claimed to have been laid out in relation to significant celestial events. The most famous is Stonehenge, the alignment of which was deliberately set to respect the midsummer sunrise and the midwinter sunset.

From the evidence before us there can be little doubt that by about 3000 BC the communities of Atlantic Europe had developed a deep understanding of the solar and lunar calendars – an understanding that could only have come from close observation and careful recording over periods of years. That understanding was monumentalized in the architectural arrangement of certain of the megalithic tombs and stone circles. What was the motivation for this we can only guess – to pay homage to the gods who controlled the heavens?; to gain from the power released on these special days?; to be able to chart the passing of the year? – these are all distinct possibilities. But perhaps there was another motive. By building these precisely planned structures, the communities were demonstrating their knowledge of, and their ability to 'contain', the phenomenon: they were entering into an agreement with the deities – a partnership – which guaranteed a level of order in the chaos and uncertainty of the natural world.

The people who made the observations and recorded them, and later coerced the community into the coordinated activity that created the remarkable array of monumental structures, were individuals of rare ability – the keepers of knowledge and the mediators between common humanity and the gods. They were essential to the wellbeing of society, and we can only suppose that society revered them.

Returning to our simplified model, it could be argued that the monuments we have been considering were a reflection of the community's engagement with the powers controlling the sky. What, then, of the chthonic deities of earth and water? There are some clues from the archaeological record. In the 3rd and 2nd millennia, a commonly observed phenomenon was the digging of pits, many of which appear to have had no utilitarian function but which often contained collections of artefacts or animal bones suggestive of deliberate deposition. The interpretation frequently put forward is that these structures represent offerings placed in the earth to propitiate the chthonic deities. One outstanding example is the shaft of mid-2nd millennium date found at Wilsford, 1.5 kilometres south-west of Stonehenge. The shaft, 1.8 metres in diameter and 30 metres deep, penetrated the chalk sufficiently to reach the water-table. The interpretation of the structure as a ritual shaft is not entirely straightforward since there was no convincing evidence of a votive deposit within the fill, and indeed a wooden bucket and length of rope found in the bottom might suggest a more prosaic explanation, but that said, even if the shaft had functioned as a well the water itself, coming from deep in the rock, would surely have been regarded as sacred. Ambivalent attitudes to wells are seen throughout time, particularly in the medieval period when many wells and springs were believed to be presided over by saints, usually females. In the prehistoric period, it is quite conceivable that any act of penetration in the soil was seen as a violation of the domain of the deities and had to be mitigated by offerings and observances.

The amount of material deliberately consigned to the earth increased dramatically throughout the late 2nd and early 1st millennia and survives now in the archaeological record as 'hoards', usually comprising collections of bronze implements. In the past, hoards of this kind were generally regarded as deposits 'hidden' with the intention later to recover them, but, while this may be so in some cases, most hoards are now thought to be offerings made to the deities. If so, they could be thought of as a tithe of a product made from materials drawn from the earth which has been returned to the earth to maintain harmony. Bronze hoards appear to increase in number through time, reaching to a crescendo of deposition in the 7th to 6th centuries. Armorica (the name given in ancient times to the part of Gaul that includes the Brittany peninsula and the area between the Seine and Loire rivers, extending down the Atlantic coast) presents an extreme case. Here, in this final stage of hoarding, more than 300 deposits comprising 40,000 or so axes have been recovered, but most of the axes were not functional. They were now made with a high lead content, which makes them too soft to use, and they had not been properly finished. The implication, then, is that the Breton axes may have been made specifically for deposition, and it is possible that the high lead content was a deliberate attempt to bulk out the metal supply so that more could be manufactured.

What factors led to the increased volume of hoarding, and to the extreme Armorican response, it is impossible to say. The suggestion that it was in some way linked to the replacement of bronze by iron as the metal of choice for tools and weapons seems too simplistic. A more likely context may be the change in agrarian productivity which seems to have taken place after the middle of the 2nd millennium. Corn-growing became increasingly important, with more of the landscape laid out as permanent fields devoted to cereal production. This development may have been a response to population growth or to an enhanced social value attached to maintaining a surplus – perhaps both – but in any event, fertility and productivity, perceived to be in the gift of the gods, would have had to have been ensured through propitiation. Could it be that the large quantities of bronze now consigned to the soil was one of the ways in which the chthonic deities were placated? As we will see later (in Chapter 3), as bronze hoarding came to an end, a new tradition of placing dedicatory deposits in disused corn storage pits began to be widely practised, continuing the tradition of gift but now in a context directly related to the wellbeing of the crop.

Alongside 'hoarding', there is a parallel tradition which involves the deposition of goods in watery contexts – in rivers, springs, and bogs. The implication is that such locations were perceived to be the liminal spaces through which it was possible for our world to communicate with the world below. A vivid example of this, though from a later period, is the sacred hot spring in the centre of Bath into which the Romans threw a range of offerings, dedicated to the goddess Sulis. Among the items consigned to the water were messages to the deity inscribed on sheets of lead calling for the goddess to act on behalf of the suppliant. Clearly the spring was a channel of communication.

Throughout prehistory a range of artefacts, mainly tools and weapons, were deposited in watery contexts. One of the earliest in Britain is the superb polished jadeite axe, originating in the western Alps, which was placed in a bog alongside a wooden trackway – the Sweet Track – built across the Somerset marshes in about 3000 BC. It must have been an object of huge social value the deposition of which was an act of great piety. We can only guess its meaning, but it is tempting to think that it was placed to ensure the safety of those using a trackway which the community had imposed upon the domain of the presiding deity.

In the 2nd and early 1st millennia, material thrown into rivers becomes increasingly common – a tradition which, as we will see, is maintained and intensified in the Iron Age. The principal items are weapons, leading to the suggestion that these might have been the spoils of battle dedicated to the gods in recognition of a victory. Some of the individual weapons may have had long histories, their fame sealed by successful use. The deposition of such an item would have been an occasion of great note.

Deposition in earth and in water – including no doubt the sea – suggests that reverence for the natural world played an important part in the belief systems of the people. It is not unlikely that other natural phenomena – a striking rocky crag or an ancient tree – were also treated with reverence, but direct archaeological evidence is generally lacking.

In addition to these natural portals to the gods, there were also man-made locations. We have already mentioned the stone circles and stone alignments found along the length of the Atlantic zone. To these we may add the remarkable circular timber monuments, like Woodhenge and Durrington Walls near Stonehenge and the Sanctuary near Avebury, composed of concentric circles of massive upright timbers which may have been similar in function to the stone circles and appear to have been built to reflect celestial alignments. And then there is the confusing scatter of enigmatic structures which enlivened the landscape from the mid-4th to mid-2nd millennia – the causewayed camps, cursus monuments, and henges, the last two categories being confined largely to the British Isles. All three were forms of enclosure, their limits defined by ditches which bounded an area, separating it from the world outside.

The causewayed enclosures, as their name implies, were characterized by discontinuous ditches and may have performed a range of functions. Some, like Windmill Hill in Wiltshire, are thought to have been meeting places used, perhaps, for ceremonial gatherings at certain times during the year. Others, like Hambledon Hill in Dorset, seem to have been places where the dead were excarnated. The portmanteau term 'henge monument' covers a variety of enclosures of different sizes and configurations. Many of them are associated with depositions, sometimes in pits, which, together with the lack of evidence of normal domestic activity, suggests some kind of ritual function. Finally, there are the cursus monuments – very long enclosures defined by parallel ditches. The largest is the Dorset Cursus, averaging 100 metres wide and 10 kilometres long. The cursus in the vicinity of Stonehenge is the same width but only 2.7 kilometres in length. How such structures functioned in the ritual landscape has long been a subject of lively debate but remains unresolved. The 18th-century antiquarian suggestion that they may have been for running events (hence the name) may not be too far-fetched.

The rich and varied ritual landscapes of Britain, Ireland, and Armorica, though different in their detail, reflect societies which, throughout the 3rd and into the 2nd millennia, were investing much of their surplus capacity in creating structures and spaces for ritual observance. Ritual sites are known in Gaul from this period, but the structural details differ and, on present evidence, there seem to be far fewer of them. Yet taken together, the conclusion must be that, wherever you were, the gods, and man's physical response to them, were never very far away.

To attempt to construct belief systems from scraps of mute archaeological evidence is a near-impossible task, but from the facts so briefly surveyed above some general observations can be made. Perhaps the most striking aspect of life in the Neolithic and Bronze Age is the high level of communal investment in the monumentalization of ritual practice through monument building, whether it be places of assembly for the living or of repose for the ancestors. That a huge amount of society's energy went into these constructions is an indication of the importance of ritual observance. Reverence for ancestors and, in the 2nd millennium, the consignment of grave goods with the body, may well reflect a belief in the continuity of spirit and some understanding of an afterlife. Finally, there can be little doubt that the celestial calendar was well understood and that it formed the structure around which the year, with its ceremonies and observances, was fashioned.

The rich fabric of prehistoric belief, revealed by the archaeological evidence especially in Britain, Ireland, and Armorica, could only have been maintained by specialists – a group with coercive authority capable of abstract thought, philosophical speculation, and scientific observation, who passed on their learning from one generation to the next. Although there was no doubt considerable regional variation, and there were changes in practice over time, the broad similarities along the whole Atlantic interface are impressive.

So, where does this lead us? Could it be that the Druids, who are known to the Classical world from the 4th century BC, had their roots deep in this prehistory – that the accumulated wisdoms which they guarded and taught were the legacy of learning and practice going back into the 2nd and 3rd millennia BC? There is nothing at all unreasonable in this suggestion, indeed there is a logic in it, but there is no way in which it can be validated: it remains at best an interesting speculation. One further observation needs to be made. Julius Caesar, as we have seen, recorded his belief that druidism originated in Britain and that those who wished to study it were advised to make a journey to the island. From where he gathered this belief and whether it was valid we will never know, but there remains the intriguing possibility that he was right. Britain was an island redolent of ancient religious practice; perhaps his informants had access to oral traditions that spoke of these times.

Chapter 3

The archaeology of religious practice at the time of the Druids

Evidence for religious belief and practice in the second half of the 1st millennium – the time when the Druids are known to have been practising – is both extensive and varied. In this chapter, we will examine something of the range of the data available for study, but we will resist the temptation to interpret it in the light of what the Classical sources tell us: the archaeological evidence must, at least for a while, be allowed to speak for itself. Its overriding message is that ritual behaviour pervaded every aspect of life.

The disposal of the dead continued to feature large, with a bewildering variety of practices varying quite markedly from place to place and time to time. At the elite level, burials were usually accompanied by a range of grave goods related to the status of the individual. In eastern Gaul and southern Germany, most elaborate burials were placed in wood-lined chambers set into the ground and were provided with a wide range of grave goods. The female burial found at Vix, in eastern France, was laid on the body of the four-wheeled vehicle that had carried her to the grave and was accompanied by a complete set of wine-drinking equipment – bronze, silver, and pottery – all imported from the Mediterranean at the end of the 6th century. A decade or so earlier, at Hochdorf near Stuttgart, a male aristocrat had been laid on a bronze couch next to his funerary cart with his bow, quiver of arrows, drinking horns, and Greek bronze cauldron close at hand. Some of his equipment was covered in gold sheeting manufactured at the time of the burial ceremony. The tradition of elite burial accompanied by vehicles, weapons, and feasting gear continued in the Marne–Moselle region into early La Tène times (5th century BC) and recurs elsewhere, in the Ardennes and Yorkshire, into the 3rd and 2nd centuries.

Individuals afforded elite burial were usually inhumed, and in Britain this tradition of inhumation continued, at least for a sector of the population, up to the time of the Roman invasion, but other burial rituals were also widely practised. Perhaps the most widespread was excarnation – the exposure of the body above ground. The principal evidence for this is the general absence of any other burial mode, the occurrence of body parts in domestic contexts, and the occasional burial of tightly wrapped bodies. The *rite de passage*, which this range of behaviour reflects, suggests that the first stage of disposal involved the exposure of the body, perhaps bound and wrapped in cloth, in a designated area set aside for excarnation. After a period of time, the bodies

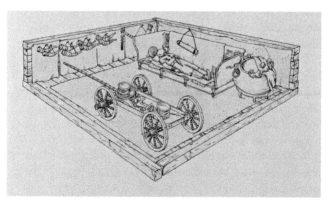

1. Reconstruction of the burial chamber of a chieftain buried with his finery beneath a barrow at Hochdorf, near Stuttgart, Germany in the late 6th century BC

were removed, either for burial in the ground, or were brought back into the settlement where, as revered ancestors, they could be reincorporated into the existence of the living. Evidence for reburial has been found at Suddern Farm in Hampshire, where a number of tightly wrapped bundles of articulated bones were interred in a small cemetery close to the settlement. Evidence in support of reincorporation comes from the large number of disarticulated bones which are found on settlement sites in south-eastern Britain and in Gaul.

Cremation was also quite widely practised, particularly after the end of the 2nd century BC in northern Gaul and south-eastern Britain. The cremated remains were usually placed in urns, sometimes accompanied by other pottery vessels, presumably containing food or drink, and occasionally by items of metal wine-drinking equipment, perhaps representing the elevated status of the deceased. In the 1st century BC and early 1st century AD, more elaborate cremation burials are found in large chambers where the ashes are accompanied by offerings of food, amphorae of wine and the ceramic and metal vessels needed in their consumption, and other items of personal equipment. Superficially these elite cremations look quite simple, but something of the potential complexities of the rituals that may be involved is well demonstrated by an elite burial of the 1st century AD found at Folly Lane just outside the Roman town of Verulamium (St Albans). Here a large chamber was dug and the corpse, together with a range of grave goods, were laid out, no doubt with the intention that they should be viewed by the mourners. Then, after an appropriate period of time, the body was removed and cremated, and the grave goods were smashed, following which the grave pit was filled in. This series of events clearly represented an orderly *process* of departure, from the moment of the individual's last breath to the completion of the rite and the closure of the tomb.

Although burial rites were varied both regionally and chronologically, the care with which the dead were put to rest is readily apparent. The provision of grave goods is a constant theme particularly among the elite. Taken all together, the evidence shows that normative death was a highly ritualized occasion which demanded adherence to ceremony. The process seems to have embedded within it the concept that the deceased passed on from life on earth to enjoy an afterlife appropriate to his or her status. The basic concepts in the late 1st millennium BC are not very different from those of the earlier prehistoric period.

The burial in the ground of a corpse, bundle of bones, or cremated ashes may well have been conceptualized within the broader context of consigning dedicatory deposits to the earth, thereby placing them in the realms of the chthonic deities. It may also be that cremated remains were thrown into rivers or lakes in a ritual parallel to the deposition of tools and weapons in watery places, but of this there is, unsurprisingly, no positive trace.

Deposition in water and earth – traditions deeply rooted in prehistory – continued throughout the 1st millennium. A surprisingly high percentage of the elite Iron Age metalwork found in Britain and Ireland – including swords, daggers, shields, helmets, and bowls – has come from rivers and bogs, one of the most prolific locations being the middle reaches of the River Thames. The tradition, which began in the middle of the 2nd millennium BC, reached a crescendo in the century before the Roman invasion. Spectacular pieces of craftsmanship like the Waterloo Bridge Helmet and the Battersea Shield demonstrate the extremes to which people would go to assuage the demands of the gods. Items like these, readily identifiable and no doubt redolent with history, must have been of enormous social value. The ending of their earthly life through acts of deposition would have been an occurrence of great moment in the history of the community.

That certain stretches of river seem to produce more artefacts than others suggests that there may have been specific locations from which the depositions were made. This is most clearly seen in the case of the lake (now a bog) of Llyn Cerrig Bach in Anglesey, from which a large hoard of Late Iron Age metalwork was recovered. The location of the finds suggests that they were thrown in from a rock platform on the lake edge. There are also examples of timber walkways built out into the water from which items were thrown. The most famous is at La Tène on Lake Neuchâtel in Switzerland from around which a large number of artefacts were recovered. Other walkways have been identified at Flag Fen near Peterborough and at Fiskerton in the River Witham. The Flag Fen platform was in use throughout the 1st millennium BC up to the Roman period. Fiskerton, which belongs to the 5th and 4th centuries, is particularly interesting in that dendrochronological studies have shown that it was repaired at regular intervals on a periodicity of 16–18 years, which suggests regular renewal perhaps related to the 19-year lunar cycle.

Depositions in the earth continued to be made throughout the 1st millennium to the time of the Roman conquest. They take many forms. The most spectacular are the hoards of torcs and other items made in precious metals, gold, silver, and electrum (an alloy of gold and silver) which are found in some number in East Anglia. The most extensively studied is the site of Snettisham in Norfolk, where a number of discrete hoards have been found comprising torcs, coins, and scrap items buried in small pits dug specifically for the purpose. All the hoards lie within an 8-hectare enclosure, which appears to have been of Roman date – some decades after the deposition of the hoards. One possibility is that it was dug to define the boundary of the territory known, in the local memory, to have been sacred to the gods.

Less spectacular, but no less dramatic, are depositions found in pits originally dug for storage purposes. Storage pits, or silos, are a feature of late 1st-millennium settlements throughout western Europe occurring particularly densely in south-eastern Britain and the adjacent regions of France and the Low Countries wherever soil conditions are such that stable pits can be dug. It is probable that the majority of the pits were used as underground silos for the storage of seed grain. Once the useful life of the pits was over, they were abandoned and in many cases given over to a secondary use as a repository for votive deposition comprising groups of artefacts, dumps of grain, joints of meat, animal carcasses in whole or in part, and human remains. These are the tangible items likely to survive in the archaeological record: it is quite conceivable that other deposits were also made, including furs, fleeces, bales of wool, fabrics, cheeses, and suchlike, all of which would leave no archaeological trace in normal conditions. It was usual for the initial deposits to be made on the pit bottoms soon after abandonment. Thereafter, by processes of natural erosion, pits were allowed to silt up but quite often secondary and tertiary deposits were added as erosion proceeded.

While there is much variety to be observed in these processes of deposition, the overall intention is clear, but what does it mean? One plausible explanation is that the primary deposits reflect propitiatory offerings made to the chthonic deities for having safely protected the seed corn during the liminal period of winter, while the subsequent deposits may be offerings made in anticipation of a successful harvest or as thanks after the harvest has been safely gathered in. For an agrarian community whose very livelihood was based on the continued fertility and productivity of the crops, the agricultural year would have been punctuated with rituals designed to placate the deities. Indeed, the practice of storing seed grain in pits may have been conditioned by the belief that the safest place for the vital seeds during the liminal period was in the realms of the earth deities.

The discovery of human remains in pits raises the difficult question of human sacrifice. Isolated bones or even articulated body parts could be explained in terms of their being the remains of ancestors brought in from the excarnation grounds and deposited as valued offerings to the gods. But entire skeletons are not infrequently found – some tightly bound, others splayed in a variety of poses on the pit bottoms. The bound remains could be ancestor bundles, but the others look more sinister as though the bodies, dead or alive, were thrown unceremoniously into the voids. In several instances, large, heavy flint nodules were dumped above the skeletons. It is tempting to regard such deposits as the result of sacrifice though, of course, other explanations are possible.

That said, there can be little doubt about the fate of Lindow Man – a body found in a bog in Cheshire. He had been hit violently on the head, had been garrotted, and had had his throat cut before being placed in the bog. His 'triple death' looks very much like ritual killing and his resting place, in a bog, would have been appropriate for a sacrificial victim.

Among the human remains found in archaeological contexts, the head has often been selected for special treatment. This is vividly demonstrated at temple sites in southern France, like Roquepertuse, where human skulls were set in niches carved into stone pillars or nailed to wooden posts. Isolated skulls are also sometimes found in pits or in defensive ditches near entrances where they might have been displayed on gates. Clearly the head was perceived to be a special body part, perhaps one that contained the power of the deceased. The longevity of the belief is demonstrated by reverence for skulls at Neolithic sites like Hambledon Hill, where human skulls were found placed at intervals along the bottom of the enclosing ditch.

While ritual behaviour seems to have pervaded all aspects of daily life, and could have been practised anywhere in the landscape, there were also specific locations set aside to serve as temples or shrines, usually defined by ditched enclosures. In the south of France, these often incorporated stone-built architecture and were provided with stone statues of gods or heroes, but more often in the north of Gaul and in Britain they were timber-built.

2. The body of a man ritually killed and buried in a bog in the 1st century AD. He was found during peat cutting at Lindow, Cheshire, England

One of the best known of the northern French temples is the multiperiod structure excavated at Gournay-sur-Aronde (Oise). The sanctuary was situated on a spur overlooking a small stream: it was first built in the 4th century BC and rebuilt on a number of occasions thereafter until the 1st century, when it was destroyed by fire and the site levelled, but its memory remained, and in the 4th century AD a Gallo-Roman shrine was built on the same spot. The central focus of the sacred site was a large oval-shaped pit containing the remains of sacrificed cattle which was set within a rectangular ditched enclosure. Over the years, the pit was associated with, and later enclosed within, a succession of timber structures, while the outer enclosure was frequently refurbished and enhanced with timber palisades. The ditch was used throughout as a place for the deposition of sacrificed materials including over 2,000 weapons and large quantities of animal remains – the result of individual acts of sacrifice spanning the life of the temple.

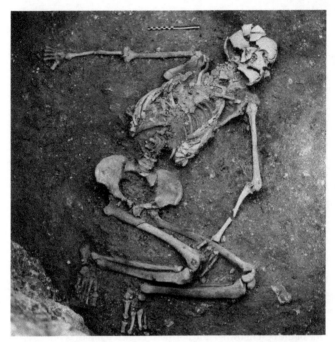

3. Body, possibly of a sacrificial victim, laid out on the bottom of a pit in the hillfort at Danebury, Hampshire, England. The pit dates to the 3rd or 2nd century BC

Gournay-sur-Aronde is characteristic of the Iron Age temples found scattered across northern Gaul and Britain. For the most part, the temple buildings are small, usually square but sometimes circular, and are almost invariably set within an enclosure defining the sacred *temenos*. In a number of cases, the temples continued in use into the Roman period, at which time they were often rebuilt in stone.

Another type of defined religious location, found extensively in western-central Europe, are the rectangular enclosures known as *viereckschanzen* which may contain timber-built shrines, burials

4. Two of the many wooden statues placed as votive offerings at the shrine of Sequana, guarding the source of the Seine at St Germain sur Seine. They date from the early Roman period and were probably placed by worshippers to draw the deities' attention to themselves and their particular ailments

and shafts, or wells, in any combination. The well-examined example from Holzhausen in Bavaria contained a small timber 'shrine' set in one corner together with three shafts up to 40 metres deep, in one of which was an upright wooden stake associated with materials identified as the decayed remains of flesh or blood. Another example excavated at Fellbach-Schminden in Baden-Württemberg contained a number of burials and a single shaft some 20 metres deep which had been lined with timber and had probably served as a well providing water for ritual purposes. When it was finally abandoned, two pottery vessels were placed on the bottom. The top of the shaft had been ornamented with elaborate wooden carvings of animals, including rampant stags and goats, which survived largely intact in the waterlogged fillings.

The *viereckschanzen* differed from the temple sites but were evidently intricately bound up with ritual behaviour perhaps related to celebrating the memory of ancestors, if we assume the burials to represent those of a lineage. The shafts with which many were furnished, if deep enough, may have provided water for ritual purposes and are clearly in the same tradition as the much earlier (2nd-millennium) shaft found at Wilsford near Stonehenge. That some of the shafts contained offerings is again an indication of the religious nature of the sites. In the case of shafts used as wells, the deposition of offerings is most likely associated with rites of closure.

We have already mentioned the significance attached to watery places as locations for deposition. One particular type of place was the spring where water from the underworld rose to flow into the land of humans. Such places were revered and many were believed to have curative properties. One of the best known lies at the source of the Seine, some 35 kilometres north-west of Dijon, where, in the Roman period, there was a thriving shrine to Sequana, goddess of the river. Excavations in a waterlogged area brought to light a remarkable collection of wooden *ex votos* in

40

the form of human or animal figurines which are thought to have been placed along a terrace wall facing the sacred area during the 1st century AD, when the old shrine was being renovated. The human figurines are a varied collection including complete figures, some wearing hooded cloaks, heads, trunks, limbs, hands, and feet. Some of the trunks are carved to give impressions of the internal organs, one of the most vivid being a representation of a rib cage with the lungs and trachea inside. There are also models of sexual organs, breasts, and eyes. The intention of the suppliants was evidently to provide the goddess, Sequana, with an unambiguous indication on which part of their anatomy she was to concentrate her curative or rejuvenating powers.

Another curative spring, at Chamalières, near Clermont-Ferrand, produced a comparable collection of wooden *ex votos* from early Roman contexts dating to the century or so following Caesar's conquest of Gaul. They represented much the same range as those from Sequana's spring, except that indications of illness and deformity are rare. However, the fact that Chamalières is a mineral water spring suggests that pilgrims were attracted there for its curative properties. The votive offerings from both springs were found in early Roman contexts. While it is possible that some of the objects survived from earlier periods, it is more likely that the practice of presenting representations to the deities is an attribute of Mediterranean culture. Even so, the veneration of the springs must go back to a more distant period.

The little wooden figurines presented to the deities are only one facet of a rich tradition of religious representational craftsmanship practised in western Europe. Wooden carvings are preserved only rarely, where suitable conditions of waterlogging allow, but given the ease of carving, one may assume that they were once widespread.

More common are sculptures in stone which reflect a varied range of traditions. One of the best-known assemblages comes from a temple site at Roquepertuse (Bouches-du-Rhône) in southern France which

5. Portico of skulls from the sanctuary of Roquepertuse, near Aix-en-Province, France, dating to the 3rd to 2nd centuries BC

dates to the 3rd century BC. What survive are the stone elements of the stone and timber architecture of a temple comprising columns, with niches carved out to contain human skulls, and a horizontal frieze carved with horses' heads and surmounted by a fearsome bird of prey poised nearby to swoop. Part of the ensemble included a carving of two conjoined heads looking in opposite directions, much like the Roman god Janus – the god of coming and going. The heads shared what is frequently referred to as a 'leaf crown' – a kind of bulbous extrusion – which frames the back of the head, common among other sculptures of this period. What it means is beyond recovery, but it would appear to reflect status in some way.

Associated with the temple were a series of large figures sitting cross-legged on the ground. These are thought to be representations of heroes, either real people or mythical beings.

Roquepertuse is not alone in southern Gaul. A similar sanctuary occurred within the oppidum of Entremont, near Aix-en-Provence, and is represented now by carved stone elements, including a pillar with representations of severed heads along its length and another piece with a realistic depiction of a severed head adjacent to niches in which real severed heads would have been placed. There were also representations of seated heroes, some holding severed heads. The emphasis on the severed head is notably prevalent in southern Gaul and may reflect a belief system particular to the area of the Celto-Ligurian tribes. It is worth remembering that it was this region of Gaul with which writers like Posidonius would have been familiar – their generalizations about the Celts may therefore have been biased to the areas they knew.

Religious sculpture is known in other parts of Europe, most particularly the region that is now southern Germany. The most spectacular of the discoveries is the life-sized sculpture in the round of a bearded man carrying a shield, found in association with the 5th-century burial at Glauberg (Hesse). The figure is shown with his head framed in an embracing 'leaf crown' comparable to that of the 'Janus' heads of Roquepertuse. The interpretation of the figure is a matter of debate. It is likely to have stood on or close to the burial mound covering a princely burial and may therefore represent the deified hero lying beneath. Statues adorned with leaf crowns have been found at other sites, including Heidelberg and Holzgerlingen, and bearded heads with leaf crowns carved in relief adorn the four sides of a highly decorated pillar found at Pfalzfeld. This recurring motif clearly had a great significance reflecting exalted – perhaps even god-like – status. The presence of these statues in the landscape would have been a reminder to all of the ever-present supernatural powers.

The leaf-crowned 'heroes' are a manifestation of the 5th to 3rd centuries. Later religious sculpture of the 2nd to 1st centuries BC tends to be more realistic and more specific. Three examples from different parts of France will illustrate the point. All three represent male figures and all wear the neck torc as a sign of high status but display other characteristics. The stone figurine from Paule (Côtes d'Armor) holds a lyre, that from Euffigneix (Haute-Marne) is embellished with a lively rendition of a powerful boar, while the seated bronze statue from Bouray (Seine-et-Oise) has hoofed feet like a deer. It is tempting to see them each as a god identifiable to the initiated by their specific attributes. Perhaps here we are seeing the local tribal deities made manifest.

The sculptures are but one aspect of a considerable corpus of iconographic material which is generally referred to as 'Celtic art', best known through the medium of decorative metalwork but also represented in designs on pottery and on wooden vessels. The 'art' originates in the 5th century in the aristocratic households of the Marne–Moselle region. It was inspired by Greco-Etruscan motifs introduced on imported metal vessels, and quickly developed into a highly original style of curvilinear design – energetic and surprising. Within the art lay embedded references and meanings impossible now to interpret, but understandable at the time and used in such a way as to communicate meaning. To take just one example – the bronze shield boss dating to the 2nd or 1st century BC, dredged from the River Thames at Wandsworth. The boss would have occupied the centre of a large rectangular shield probably of wood or leather. It was circular, with a central protuberance around which was a flowing pattern of tendrils created in repoussé with infillings by engraving. A careful look at the pattern shows that it is composed of two heavily stylized birds with outstretched wings. A warrior facing the shield held by an opponent might suddenly have seen the curvilinear motifs shift into focus and the two great birds of prey emerge from the boss. He would have understood the message. In a story told by Livy of the Celtic invasion of Italy, there is a vignette of a combat between two Celts. As they approach, a huge bird of prey lands on the helmet of one of the contestants. The other, seeing it, is paralysed by fear, knowing that the gods are on the side of his opponent and are about to devour him. Perhaps the bird of prey on the temple architrave at Roquepertuse had a similar effect on those who approached the temple.

The story shows the power of the message – and Celtic art carried those messages. It was enigmatic and constantly shifting: images could appear and disappear. Nothing was ever as it seemed.

No convincing narrative art of the period has survived, with the possible exception of the famous silver Gundestrup cauldron found in a bog near Roevemosen in Denmark. The cauldron is a puzzling piece. Stylistically, it shares all the characteristics of Thracian workmanship, and yet it depicts material culture that is Celtic – war trumpets, rectangular shields, animal-crested helmets, and torcs. One plausible explanation is that it was made in Bulgaria by Thracian craftsmen as a gift for a chief of one of the Celtic tribes living nearby, by some entirely indecipherable process ending up in the Danish bog as an offering to the local gods. The fascination of the cauldron lies in the complex scenes it depicts on its two sets of repoussé decorated plaques, one set facing outwards, the other facing inwards. One of the inner scenes centres on a seated figure, evidently a god, who wears a torc and an antler head-dress and holds a torc in one hand and a serpent in the other while animals gather around. Another of the inner scenes shows a troop of warriors, some mounted, others on foot, approaching a large figure who is busy depositing a smaller figure head-first into a large container while an excited dog scampers around. Tempting though it is to offer explanations – and many have been offered – there is little that can be said with any degree of certainty beyond simple description. Nor can we be sure that it is 'Celtic' traditions that are being illustrated

6. Scene from the silver-gilt cauldron of the 2nd or 1st century BC
found in a bog at Gundestrup, Denmark. The large figure appears to be
depositing a sacrifice in a cauldron

rather than those of the Thracian world. But that said, the scenes evidently involve ritual behaviour and remind us of the complexity of the belief systems seldom accessible through archaeological evidence alone.

We saw in the last chapter how, through accurate experiment over a period of time, the rhythms of the lunar and solar cycles had been charted and monuments constructed to 'capture' major celestial events. All this had been achieved by the beginning of the 3rd millennium: thereafter, the knowledge would have been passed from generation to generation through oral learning. The extent of that knowledge at the end of the 1st millennium BC is vividly demonstrated by the surviving pieces of a large bronze calendar found at Coligny (Ain) in eastern France. The calendar, thought to have dated to the late 2nd or early 1st century BC, had been broken up and buried in a Gallo-Roman temple. It records 62 months of a 5-year cycle displayed in 16 columns each of 4 consecutive months, except for columns 1 and 9, each of which comprises 2 normal months and 1 intercalary month. Each month was of 29 or 30 days, and each was identified with the name followed by MAT(U) for the 30-day months and ANM(ATU) for the 29-day months. Since *matu* means 'complete', while *anmatu* means 'incomplete', the word presumably relates to the length of each month, but the words can also mean 'good' and 'bad', and might therefore be an indicator of whether the months are propitious or not. Each month is divided into two parts after the 15th day with the word ATENOUX, which signifies the end of the light half and the beginning of the dark period. Within each month, certain days are labelled as 'inharmonious'.

Coligny is a lunar calendar in that the passage of time is measured by nights rather than days. It was probably used to cover a 30-lunar-year cycle with the beginning of each year starting with the 6th lunar month. By manipulating the intercalary months and other adjustments, the lunar calendar could be made to coincide with the solar calendar.

7. Detail of the fragmentary bronze calendar found at Coligny, Ain, France. The calendar, probably from the 1st century AD, lists 62 months of 29 or 30 days each and indicates seasonal celebrations and propitious times

The calendar is, by any standards, a remarkable achievement representing the culmination of study going back over very many generations. Its very complexity demanded that it be committed to a more permanent form using the Latin alphabet, but this need not imply any significant input from the Mediterranean world. There is no reason to suppose other than that the calendar was the product of the indigenous inhabitants of Atlantic Europe.

We have laid out, albeit in a very summary form, a range of archaeological data relevant to the intellectual life and belief systems of the inhabitants of Gaul and Britain in the five centuries or so before the Roman invasion. The data are much richer and more varied than those of the preceding prehistoric period, and yet there are many themes in common: the importance of offerings placed in the ground or in watery contexts; the digging of deep shafts reaching towards the underworld; complex burial rites involving grave goods and the consigning of the dead to the sky and the earth; the significance of the human skull; and the careful measurement of lunar and solar time to chart the passage of the seasons and to programme ceremony. There can be little doubt that the belief systems evident in the last four centuries or so of the 1st millennium BC – the time of the historic Druids – were the result of a *longue durée* of development and refinement spanning several millennia. The druidic class, then, were the inheritors of ancient wisdoms.

Chapter 4

Enter the Druids:
the first contacts

In Chapter 1, we briefly outlined how we have come to learn about the Druids using the tantalizing scraps of information contained in the surviving Greek and Roman sources. The material is, to say the least, constrained and difficult to deal with: it is subject to biases introduced by the original writers; it incorporates observations made over many centuries and covering a wide geographical region; often what survives has been repeated third or fourth hand from some earlier text no longer extant; and, even more limiting, the record is very fragmentary. To write an objective account of druidism is therefore difficult, but therein lies the fascination of the subject. It is necessary first to untangle the complex process of transmission and then to try to penetrate the minds of the authors, the better to understand their limitations and their biases.

As we have seen in Chapter 1, the generally accepted view is that there are two broad traditions in Classical writing about the Druids – the Posidonian tradition and the Alexandrian tradition to which may be added the views of people writing during the time of the Roman Empire. While this is broadly true, the situation is a little more complex and perhaps a more objective way to approach the sources is in terms of the chronological order in which observations were made and the raw data entered the stream of available knowledge. The earliest observations of native behaviour were made by Greeks who were settling the coastal regions of southern Gaul from 600 BC and exploring the hinterland. Later, in the 2nd and early 1st centuries BC, as the Roman world became more involved in the affairs of southern Gaul, more was learned, while the conquest of Gaul and, later, Britain provided further opportunities to study the social structure and belief systems of the newly conquered peoples. Thus the three impact phases each generated a different tradition, which may be defined as:

- the Greek tradition (which fed into the Alexandrian tradition);
- the Late Republican tradition (incorporating what has been called the Posidonian tradition);
- the Imperial tradition.

In this chapter we will consider the Greek tradition, leaving the other two for discussion in Chapter 5.

The foundation of the colony of Massalia (Marseilles) around 600 BC by Greeks, from the eastern Greek city of Phocaea on the west coast of Anatolia, marked the beginning of formal relationships between the Greek world and the barbarian inhabitants of western Europe. It was the culmination of a period of exploration lasting three or four decades which saw Greek entrepreneurs probe the Mediterranean coasts of Gaul and Iberia and sail through the Pillars of Hercules (the Straits of Gibraltar) to trade with the Tartessians at their main port, now modern Huelva. The foundation of Massalia was quickly followed by the establishment of colonies at Agatha (Agde) and Emporion (Ampurias), encircling the Golfe du Lion; later, new colonies were set up along the coast to the east as far as Nicaea (Nice). Along this long coastal interface Greek settlers will have come into direct contact with native religious practices which, as we have seen, saw the construction of temples lavishly adorned with human heads.

The Greek colonial settlements were nodes of information exchange, and it was from here that eastern Greek historians like the 6th-century Hecataeus of Miletos and the 5th-century Herodotus would have learned of the Celts. They were also places from which expeditions were mounted into the unknown. Shadowy figures like Midacritus and Euthymenes sailed out into the Atlantic to explore the coasts of Iberia and Africa in search of resources and brought back stories of strange barbarians to share with their incredulous fellows in the comfort of the Mediterranean harbour towns. Others explored the hinterland of Gaul. One of these was Pytheas of Massalia who, towards the end of the 4th century, followed the old tin route across Gaul, via the Garonne river and the Gironde, to the Atlantic and then took ship northwards, visiting the tin-producing lands of Armorica and Cornwall before circumnavigating Britain, visiting inland areas as he went. It is even possible that he reached Iceland and may have crossed the North Sea to see first hand the coast of Jutland from which the much-prized amber came. He eventually made his way back to Massalia and there, around 320 BC, wrote an account of his remarkable journey called *On the Ocean*. The book no longer survives, but it was much quoted by later Mediterranean writers as the principal source on the wild north-western extremities of Europe. The first person to quote Pytheas was Dicaearchus of Messene, a pupil of Aristotle active around 326–296 BC, but *On the Ocean* was also well known to a writer of central importance to our story, Timaeus of Tauromenium (in Sicily), whose floruit was between 330 and 280.

Timaeus wrote a *History* which was well known to later writers like Cicero and Pliny. Indeed, Pliny actually acknowledges his debt to Timaeus as a source of information about Britain and the North Sea – information that must ultimately have derived from Pytheas. It is also highly likely that another Sicilian writer, Diodorus, also used Timaeus' *History* for information about the north-western barbarians, though he does not acknowledge his source.

Another early writer who quoted extensively from Pytheas was Eratosthenes of Cyrene, who was in charge of the famous library of Alexandria from about 234 to 196 BC and there wrote three books, the *Geographica*, no doubt consulting Pytheas' *On the Ocean*, which would have been housed in the library. It was from the writings of Eratosthenes that the later writer Strabo (c. 64 BC–AD 24) learned of Pytheas' observations in the west, quoting them in his own work, usually with ridicule and derision.

To sum up so far – first-hand observations on Gaul and Britain, made by Pytheas towards the end of the 4th century, are known to have been transmitted either directly or indirectly through the works of Timaeus and Eratosthenes, to the later writers Strabo, Pliny, Cicero, and probably Diodorus Siculus, all of whom – though themselves Mediterranean-based – offered descriptions of the Celts and Druids of north-western Europe. It is quite possible, therefore, that some, perhaps most, of their information about the Druids derived from Pytheas. To this we shall return later.

Another Greek source of potential relevance to our story was Hecataeus of Abdera – an historian and philosopher writing in the late 4th century BC. One of his lost works, *On the Hyperboreans*, is quoted extensively by Diodorus Siculus, and it may have been from Hecataeus that Strabo and Pliny also gleaned their information on the Hyperboreans, who were a semi-mythical people believed to inhabit the far north-west. Diodorus is quite specific:

> in the region beyond the land of the Celts [Gaul] there lies in the
> ocean an island no smaller than Sicily. This island…is situated to
> the north and is inhabited by the Hyperboreans who are called by
> that name because their home is beyond the point where the north
> wind blows.

Apollo was worshipped there in 'a notable temple adorned with many offerings and circular in shape'. He goes on to say that the people were friendly and were visited by the Greeks, who left behind votive offerings.

Superficially, this sounds like a reference to Britain or to one of the neighbouring smaller islands (if reference to the size of Sicily is ignored). Mention of Apollo implies that it was the moon that was revered, while the circularity of the temple could refer to one of the many stone circles found in the north-west.

Diodorus (still quoting Hecataeus) continues:

> They say that the moon, as viewed from the island, appears but
> a little distance above the earth…The account is also given
> that the god visits the island every nineteen years, the period in
> which the return of the stars to the same place in the heavens is
> accomplished;…At the time of this appearance of the god he both
> plays on the cithara (lyre) and dances continuously through from
> the vernal equinox until the rising of the Pleiades.
>
> (*Hist.* II, 47)

While all this may be little more than fancy, it has the ring of factual substance behind it and one modern writer on archaeoastronomy, Aubrey Burl, has suggested that the visit of the moon every 19 years reflects the 18.61-year lunar cycle experienced in the north. Moreover, the appearance of the moon skimming across the horizon will happen only at a latitude of 58°N. The reference to the spring equinox and the Pleiades (the Seven Sisters) is more difficult to interpret, but it could refer to the observation that the moon would appear to skim the horizon from the spring equinox (21 March) until the Celtic ceremony of Beltane (1 May), which is the first moment when the Pleiades are visible in the east at their dawn rising. Burl would argue that, taken together, the astronomical observations reported by Diodorus could all be accommodated on the island of Lewis, where the great stone circle and alignments of Callanish are situated.

If we accept that Hecataeus was recording the detail of moon worship in the British Isles, how could he possibly have learned of the fact, and with so much circumstantial detail? One possibility is that his source was Pytheas, who had probably sailed up the west coast of Britain in his circumnavigation. There is also quite strong evidence to suggest that Pytheas may have stopped at Lewis en route, to make one of his midsummer sun height measurements which enabled him to estimate the distance he had travelled from his home in Massalia.

There is much speculation in all this, but the Hyperborean story stands a good chance of being the earliest surviving record of the lunar-based religion of the barbarians of the north-west at the time of the Druids.

There can be little doubt that the stories brought back by Pytheas, and perhaps by other travellers about whom we know nothing, telling of the religious behaviour of the Gauls and Britons, became common knowledge among Mediterranean scholars in the 3rd and 2nd centuries. Either directly or through secondary sources like Timaeus and Eratosthenes, knowledge of the Druids spread. They are mentioned in *Magicas* (a book wrongly ascribed to Aristotle) dating to c. 200 BC and in Sotion's *Succession of Philosophers* (c. 190 BC), and it is from this accumulation of secondary and tertiary sources that a cluster of later Greek writers glean their information – men like Alexander Cornelius Polyhistor (born c. 105 BC), Timagenes (1st century BC), Posidonius (c. 135–c. 50 BC), Dio Chrysostom (AD 40–c. 120), and Diogenes Laertus (3rd century AD). They, in turn, were used as sources by Christian writers, Clement of Alexandria (c. AD 150–c. 216), Cyril of Alexandria (early 5th century), and Stephanus of Byzantium (early 7th century).

All these later writers were academic encyclopaedists recycling information from the works of others preserved in libraries, but they are of particular value in that they provide a direct line back to the lost first-hand accounts of the Greek explorers. Socrates gives an amusing account of the processes of research among contemporary scholars:

> Together with my friends I unroll and go through the treasures which the wise men of old have bequeathed to us in their books and if we come across anything good we excerpt it.

It was in this way that scraps of knowledge were recycled and transmitted. Although our later sources are often frustrating in their brevity, it is to these armchair scholars, working away assiduously in their libraries, that we owe our knowledge of the first glimpses of the Druids.

What stands out from these early accounts is the respect the Greek writers clearly had for the Druids: the emphasis is on the Druids as philosophers – men who ranked high among the thinkers in the barbarian world outside the narrow Greek sphere. They are listed among the wise men of the world – the Egyptians, Assyrians, Bactrians, Persians, and Indians – men of honour and justice, the philosophers of the people. What is of particular interest is that a distinction is made between the Galatai (Gauls) who had *druidae* (Druids) and the Celts who were served by *philosophati* (philosophers). This may simply reflect the general confusion that existed over the nomenclature of the west European barbarians, since the names 'Gauls' and 'Celts' were often used interchangeably. Caesar gives some insight into these matters when, in describing the peoples of Gaul, he refers to them as people 'we call Gauls', adding that they called themselves Celts. Another possibility is that use of the two names could reflect an ethnic division between the inhabitants of the region.

Dio Chrysostom, a Greek Stoic rhetorician writing at the end of the 1st century AD, gives more detailed information:

The Celts appointed Druids, who likewise were versed in the art
of seers and other forms of wisdom without whom kings were not
permitted to adopt or plan any course so that it was that those who
ruled and the kings became their subordinates and instruments of
their judgment.

(Oratio xlix)

We should, however, remember that Dio Chrysostom was highly
critical of the Roman rulers at the time and was conjuring up a
vision of a 'golden age' when power lay with the wise.

This theme, of Druids as philosophers, is also taken up by Strabo.
He distinguishes three classes of men of special honour, the Bards
(singers and poets), Vates (augurs), and the Druids, and goes on
to say:

The Druids, in addition to the science of nature, study also
moral philosophy. They are believed to be the most just of men
and are therefore entrusted with the decisions of cases affecting
either individuals or the public...These men, as well as other
authorities, have pronounced that men's souls and the universe are
indestructible though times of fire or water may prevail.

(Geog. IV, IV, 4)

The same point is made by Diodorus Siculus when he says:

They have also certain philosophers and theologians who are
treated with special honour, whom they call Druids.

(Hist. V, 31, 3)

Julius Caesar also stresses the power of the Druids. He reiterates
the view that they believe that the soul does not perish but passes
from one body to another, and goes on to add:

They hold long discussions about the heavenly bodies and their
movements, about the size of the universe and the earth, about the

nature of the physical world and about the power and properties of
the immortal gods, subjects in which they also give instructions to
their pupils.

(Gallic Wars VI, 14)

While Strabo, Diodorus, and Caesar have much more to say on
the functions of Druids, derived from later observations, it is
interesting to see in their writings, themes which they, together
with the later Alexandrian writers, may have gleaned from
the earlier Greek texts – the Druids were wise philosophers,
they believed in the transference of the soul, and they studied
astronomy and nature.

The Celtic belief in the immortal soul intrigued the Greek
writers. It was entirely contrary to the commonly held Greek
view, but it conformed closely to the beliefs of the 6th-century
philosopher Pythagoras of Samos. So extraordinary was
this idea to the Greek mind that it was not unreasonable for
observers to try to relate the Druids to the Pythagoreans.
Hippolytus, a 3rd-century AD Christian writer, tells a story of
how the Druids had 'profoundly examined the Pythagorean
philosophy', learning of it from Zalmoxis, a Thracian ex-slave
of Pythagoras. He goes on to say that the Celts honour them
[the Druids] as prophets 'because they can foretell matters by
the cyphers and numbers, according to the Pythagorean skill'.
Hippolytus was using sources which may have gone back to the
3rd century BC. An alternative view, probably also current at the
time and reported much later by Clement of Alexandria, was
that Pythagoras and the Greeks had acquired their views from
the Gauls. Neither scenario is likely to be true. Belief in the
transmigration of the soul was (and still is) widespread – that
it was given such prominence by the Greek writers was simply
because of its novelty to them. The archaeological evidence
of burial, which we have examined in previous chapters, is
consistent with such a view: the deceased were equipped to
move into a new life.

The idea that the Druids were astronomers – observers of 'the heavenly bodies and their movements', men who could be compared with *Magi* of the Persians and the *Chaldaei* of the Assyrians – is also borne out by the archaeological evidence. We have seen that a knowledge of celestial phenomena was already well advanced by the beginning of the 3rd millennium BC, and the famous Coligny calendar of the 1st century is not unreasonably assumed to be a product of druidic knowledge designed for their use in controlling the annual ceremonies and foretelling celestial events. The calendar, as we have seen, was a lunar device which conforms to Caesar's observation that the Celts calculated time by counting nights 'and in calculating birthdays and the new moon and the New Year their unit of reckoning was the night followed by day'. The Elder Pliny supports this: 'for it is by the moon that they [the Druids] measure their months and years and also their eras of 30 years'. The Coligny calendar is believed by some to be a device for calculating within 30-year periods.

The importance of time, and in particular choosing appropriate and propitious times for significant events, is nowhere better demonstrated than in Pliny's famous account of cutting the mistletoe. This is the only description of a druidic ceremony to survive and incidentally throws valuable light on druidic knowledge of natural lore.

> The Druids...hold nothing more sacred than the mistletoe and the tree on which it grows provided that it is the oak. They choose groves of oak for the sake of the tree alone and they never perform any sacred rite unless they have a branch of it.... They think that everything that grows on it is sent from heaven by the god himself. Mistletoe however is rarely found on the oak and, when it is, it is gathered with a great deal of ceremony, if possible on the sixth day of the moon...They choose this day because, although the moon has not yet reached half-size it already has considerable influence. They call the mistletoe by the name that means all healing.

In this preamble the importance of timing is stressed, though some leeway is given. By controlling the knowledge of the accurate measurement of time the Druids held power, thereby excluding the uninitiated. Once again we see the importance of the moon in these ceremonies. Pliny's account continues with details of the ritual:

> They prepare a ritual sacrifice and feast under the tree, and lead in two white bulls whose horns are bound for the first time on this occasion. A priest attired in a white vestment ascends the tree and, with a golden sickle, cuts [the mistletoe] which is caught in a white cloth. Then next they sacrifice the victims praying that god will make his gift propitious to those to whom he has given it. They believe that if given in a drink [the mistletoe] will give fertility to any barren animal and that it is a remedy against all poisons.
>
> (*Nat. Hist.* XVI, 95)

Later Pliny goes on to discuss other herbs which, so long as they are collected under the appropriate conditions, possessed a range of curative properties: selago (sabine), for example, would ward off evil and cure eye diseases, while samolos (a marsh plant) offered cattle protection against various diseases.

Where did Pliny, writing in the middle of the 1st century AD, learn of this fascinating rite? He does not give his source, but since it appears not to have been recorded by Posidonius, the possibility is that his information came directly from the earlier Greek tradition, possibly via Timaeus or Polyhistor, both of whom Pliny is known to have used as sources. That the transmitter may have been Polyhistor is hinted at by the fact that he is quoted by Pliny as the authority on oak trees and mistletoe and also upon varieties of acorns. Perhaps it was Polyhistor, himself using earlier Greek sources, who had gathered together details of druidic natural lore and practice in his own work, now lost.

One further point needs to be considered. In referring to oak trees, Pliny tells us that the name of the Druids comes from the

Greek word for oak – δρύς. If so, the second element may derive from the root *wid-* (to know), the full name thus approximating to 'those with knowledge of the oak'. Another suggestion sometimes offered, that it means 'those with very great knowledge', though possible, is less likely.

What we have learned of the Druids from sources that may reasonably be linked back to earlier Greek writings – that they were a powerful intellectual elite with a philosophy centred on the transmigration of the soul, and that they were the keepers of astronomical and herbal wisdoms – is comparatively limited, but these were the distillations made by those compiling encyclopaedic works. Stories of the cutting of the mistletoe and of the moon-worshipping Hyperboreans – vivid anecdotes that would have enlivened the texts of the original observers – have so rarely survived. To the Greek world, then, the Druids were the wise men who controlled the lives and wellbeing of 'noble savages'. As such, they deserved respect: they were, after all, neighbours and trading partners. It was only later, in the 1st century BC and 1st century AD, when the Mediterranean world of the Romans came into direct contact and conflict with the Celtic barbarians, that a rather different picture of druidism began to emerge.

Chapter 5

Altars steeped in human blood

The coastal zone of southern France between the Alpes Maritimes and the Pyrenees is, for the most part, an area of fertile lowlands, easy of access and, in the 2nd and 1st centuries BC, densely populated with the communities living in defended hill towns. Two major rivers, the Rhône and the Aude, flow through it to the sea. Both were major routes, the Rhône providing easy access northwards into the heart of west-central Europe, the Aude offering a route westwards, via the Carcassonne Gap, to the Garonne and the Gironde estuary and to the Atlantic Ocean beyond. Both of these routes were long established and along them a range of commodities flowed, in both directions, linking the Mediterranean and the barbarian hinterland. Access by sea was not easy since the coastal strip was fringed by sand and gravel bars caused by longshore drift, behind which extensive marshes had developed, and the Rhône had created an alluvial delta, the Camargue, scattered with lakes and marshland. But entrepreneurial Greeks had sought out safe havens for their port cities – Nicaea, Antipolis, Olbia, Tauroention, and Massalia – extending around the mountainous coast to the east of the Rhône delta, and Agatha, Rhode, and Emporion to the west.

From the 6th century BC, the Greek colonial ports – self-governing city states – developed, providing the essential nodes through which trade and exchange were articulated. They were not the centres of aggressive land-hungry colonists but simply self-contained ports-of-trade on the fringes of an alien hinterland – rather in the mode of Hong Kong and Macao. Immediately inland a few Hellenized towns developed – places such as St Blaise, Glanon, and Lattes – but beyond that native settlements continued to flourish on their traditional hilltop locations, though many of them, including the extensively excavated examples of Ensérune, Nages, and Entremont, had adopted elements of architecture and planning learned from the Greek coastal ports.

The indigenous population was divided into a number of tribes who were referred to as Celts or Ligurians. The divide is not clear, but Ligurians seems to be the general name applied to those in the east of the region, now the Alpes Maritimes. The traditional stories told about the foundation of Massalia specifically refer to the natives encountered by the colonial expedition as Celts. While the material culture of the indigenous communities living within easy reach of the Greek cities was influenced to different degrees by Mediterranean culture, native beliefs and behaviour were little affected. As we have seen, the cult of the severed head was widely practised among communities living barely 40 kilometres from Massalia.

From the end of the 3rd century BC, Roman interest in southern Gaul began to intensify. The principal reason was the growing conflict between Rome and Carthage following the establishment of a Carthaginian power base in south-eastern Iberia. An agreement was reached that the River Ebro divided the Carthaginian interests to the south-east from the Roman interests to the north-west, but it was short-lived and in 218 BC Rome declared war on Hannibal. The Second Punic War, as it became known, culminated in the west with the surrender of Gades (Cadiz) to the Roman army in 206. With Rome now firmly in control of the south-east of the Iberian peninsula, the territory could be organized into two provinces – Hither Spain and Further

Spain. Now attention turned to the subjugation of the warlike tribes of the interior, and it was not until 133 BC, when the native stronghold of Numantia was destroyed, that some semblance of peace was established.

The impact of these Iberian campaigns on southern Gaul was considerable. During the Second Punic War, Roman and Carthaginian armies passed through the region, and after the war the coastal routes were regularly used by the Roman army to send supplies and reinforcements to the Iberian conflict zone. Along these same routes new governors and their entourages would have passed, together with traders eager to open up the new markets and to bring booty back to Rome. The constant flow of people and material through southern Gaul in the late 3rd and 2nd centuries BC must have had an impact on indigenous communities, even though the flow of traffic would have kept to the Greek cities: it would also have made the Roman audience more aware of Celtic barbarian culture, not least because the native hill tribes soon began to realize that the Roman supply columns and the Greek ports offered profitable targets for raiding bands. The eastern part of the route, where the Alpes Maritimes came close to the sea, was particularly unsafe. The baggage trains of governors en route to Spain were attacked in 189 and 173, and in 181 and 154 the Massaliots appealed to Rome for help against Ligurian attacks on the coastal cities. Armies were sent to drive back the raiders but with little lasting effect.

In 125, the problem escalated. This time the Saluvii – immediate neighbours of Massalia – urged on by increasingly belligerent tribes in the Massif Central and the Rhône valley, began to pose a serious threat to the city. Roman consular armies were sent, but this time they were here to stay. The Saluvian capital of Entremont was destroyed in 123 and a permanent military base was established nearby at Aquae Sextiae (Aix-en-Provence). The next year the war was taken deep into the barbarian hinterland along the Rhône valley, culminating, in 121, with a decisive victory for the Romans against a Celtic confederation led by the Allobroges and the Arverni fought out somewhere close to the confluence of the Isère and Rhône.

In the aftermath of the war of 125–121, southern Gaul became the Roman province of Transalpina. A citizen colony of Narbo Martius (Narbonne) was founded in 118 with a new market town of Forum Domitii not far from the old Greek port of Agatha. All the new establishments were linked by a major highway – the Via Domitia – joining Italy to Iberia.

But all was by no means peaceful. From 109, a hoard of northern barbarians – the Cimbri and Teutones – caused havoc in the new province, until their final destruction in two battles, at Aquae Sextiae in 102 and Vercellae in northern Italy in 101. The unrest encouraged the Volcae to rebel, slaughtering a Roman garrison at Tolosa (Toulouse). This resulted in a brutal counterattack by the Romans, ending in the sacking and permanent occupation of the city in 106. It was during this campaign that the Roman general Caepio destroyed a Celtic temple and took for himself its treasure of gold and silver. In writing of these events, Strabo mentions that the Celts had deposited large quantities of silver and gold in lakes and that the Romans now sold off the lakes so that entrepreneurs could recover the loot. These were, presumably, ritual deposits which the Celts had dedicated to their deities. The profanity of the Roman act was deeply resented.

But troubles did not end there. In 90, the Saluvii rebelled, and there were uprisings in the province in 83. Then followed a period of unrest when Transalpina was caught up in the power struggles between Roman warlords operating in Italy and Iberia. The 60s saw further native unrest caused by the exploitative attitudes of successive Roman governors. The focus of this was the Allobroges of the Rhône valley and the troubles required successive military expeditions to quell.

In summary, we can say that the period 218–60 BC saw the Roman world take an increasingly active role in the affairs of the Celts and Ligurians of southern Gaul. Most of the native people for much of the time were allies and trading partners. The early conflicts were largely the result of small-scale raiding: the few major confrontations were restricted to the further frontiers in the upper reaches of the Rhône valley and the valley of the Garonne. Transalpina must have been, for many Romans, an exciting place – a frontier territory full of opportunity where there was money to be made through trade and exploitation – but also a place of fascination where the mêlée of peoples, native Celts, old Greek families, and new brash Italians, jostled together, communicating in a mixture of languages, all attempting to accommodate to the fast-changing world. To Mediterranean scholars with an interest in ethnography, Transalpina offered a laboratory for study.

One man who took up the challenge was Posidonius (c. 135–c. 50 BC), a Greek Stoic philosopher and polymath born in Apamaea in Syria. In 95 BC, aged about 30, he settled in Rhodes, one of the great centres of intellectual activity at the time, and from there he travelled widely throughout the Roman world collecting information for his numerous and varied studies. Most of his writing would have been done in Rhodes, where he had access to one of the world's best libraries, no doubt holding the works of Pytheas, Timaeus, and other major primary sources, but of his extensive output, including his great work *Histories*, nothing now survives other than as quotations in the writings of other authors.

Among his travels, Posidonius visited Gaul, during the period 95–50 BC, observing and recording the beliefs and lives of the Celts and tracing for himself the famous journey which Hannibal had made through the Alps. From what has survived of his writings, it is evident that he was a shrewd and industrious observer, well aware that he was viewing a people in a state of rapid transition. On several occasions, he was careful to tell his readers that a particular practice belonged to 'former times'.

This raises the interesting question of whether he was simply recording the recollections of an informant or contrasting his own observations with accounts he had read in earlier sources. It is seldom possible to distinguish his first-hand observations from his library research, except where he cites a source.

We cannot, however, assume that Posidonius was an impartial reporter. He was a Stoic philosopher who believed in idealizing primitive people, contrasting their innocent simple state to the corruption of the civilized world. The Stoic philosopher Seneca, writing in the first half of the 1st century AD, actually said, 'In that age we call Golden Posidonius believes that those who ruled were confined to the wise.' A later writer, Athenaeus (fl. c. AD 200), refers to the 'stoic philosopher Posidonius describing many customs of many peoples in his *Histories* which work he composed in accordance with his philosophical convictions'. So the warning is clear – when Posidonius describes the Celts and the Druids, he does so through the eyes of one believing in the 'noble savage'.

Although the original writings of Posidonius do not survive, he was much quoted by later writers, though rarely with acknowledgement. The scholar J. J. Tierney, who some 50 years ago attempted to reconstruct the Celtic ethnography of Posidonius, argued that much of what was said of the Celts by Strabo, Diodorus Siculus, Athenaeus, and Caesar was derived directly from the lost *Histories*. This is certainly so of Athenaeus, who explicitly says he is quoting from the twenty-third book of Posidonius' *Histories*, and there are certain close similarities in the accounts of Diodorus Siculus and Strabo which suggest that they too used this source, though not necessarily exclusively. Caesar poses a different problem. He may have been aware of the Posidonian account, but he is also likely to have gleaned much from personal observations made as he fought his way through Gaul. For this reason, we will deal with his contribution separately later.

If we accept that Athenaeus, Strabo, and Diodorus Siculus all relied heavily on Posidonius as a source for the Celts, then what they say must be based largely on a text composed in the first half of the 1st century BC by a scholar who had visited the area and had seen the rapidly changing society for himself. While his philosophical stance may have influenced his presentation, his observations are likely to have been accurately made from real-life situations.

What then can we learn of the religious systems of southern Gaul in the early 1st century BC?

Strabo's text is the fullest and offers a detailed insight into the intellectual elite of Celtic society. Among all the tribes, he says, there are three classes of men comprising the elite: the Bards, the Vates, and the Druids: 'The Bards are singers and poets; the Vates the interpreters of sacrifice and the natural philosophers; while the Druids, in addition to the science of nature, study also moral philosophy.' He then goes on to provide details of the judicial powers of the druidic class:

> They are believed to be the most just of men and are therefore entrusted with the decision of cases affecting either individuals or the public; indeed in former times they arbitrated in war and brought to a standstill the opponents when about to draw up in line; and murder cases have been mostly entrusted to their decision.

He concludes with a general observation that they believe the souls of men to be indestructible.

Diodorus, presumably using the same Posidonian text as Strabo, offers a little more detail. The Bards, he says, are lyric poets: 'They sing to the accompaniment of instruments resembling lyres, sometimes a eulogy and sometimes a satire.' The second class, the Vates (whom Diodorus calls 'seers'), are men thought to be 'worthy of high praise' who, 'by their augural observances

68

and by the sacrifice of sacrificial animals can foretell the future and they hold all the people subject to them'. Then there are the Druids, 'philosophers and theologians who are treated with special honour'. He goes on to say that no-one would offer sacrifice without a philosopher being present since only a philosopher can communicate with the gods. The description ends with a comment about how they can intercede to stop battles, concluding 'Thus even among the most savage barbarians anger yields to wisdom' – a nice evocation of the 'noble savage'.

This same tripartite division of wise men is also echoed by the late 4th-century AD writer Ammianus Marcellinus whose source was the 1st-century AD Alexandrian historian Timagenes. Timagenes, like Strabo and Diodorus, may also have derived his knowledge of the Celts from Posidonius.

The Posidonian tradition, then, makes a clear distinction between the three classes of wise men. It is a distinction that we will see later in the Irish vernacular texts, in which the three classes are named as *baird*, *filidh*, and *druïdh*. The distinction between the Vates and Druids is worth emphasizing. The Vates were those with powers to foretell the future through augury and whose duties included carrying out the sacrifices. They were directly equivalent to the *haruspices* of the Etruscans and Romans. The Druids, on the other hand, were the philosophers and the intermediaries between man and the gods, as well as being the ultimate justices and being skilled in 'the science of nature'.

Diodorus adds further details about the Vates:

> When enquiring into matters of great import they have a strange and incredible custom; they devote to death a human being and stab him with a dagger in the region above the diaphragm, and when he has fallen they foretell the future from his fall and from the convulsions of his limbs and, moreover from the spurting of

the blood, placing their trust in some ancient and long-continued observation of these practices.

(Hist. V, 31, 3)

Strabo mentions the same practice adding:

There are also other accounts of their human sacrifices; for they used to shoot men down with arrows, and impale them in the temples, or making a large statue of straw and wood, throw into it cattle and all sorts of wild animals and human beings, and thus make a burnt offering.

(Geog. IV, IV, 4)

The theme of human sacrifice is also taken up by Julius Caesar:

The Gauls believe the power of the immortal gods can be appeased only if one human life is exchanged for another, and they have sacrifices of this kind regularly established by the community. Some of them have enormous images made of wickerwork, the limbs of which they fill with living men; these they set on fire and the men perish, enveloped in the flames. They believe that the gods prefer it if the people executed have been caught in the act of theft or armed robbery or some other crime, but when the supply runs out they even go to the extent of sacrificing innocent men.

(BG VI, 16)

There is sufficient similarity between the three quotations to suggest that all three writers were using the same source material, which we may assume to be Posidonius. Strabo, writing at the beginning of the 1st century AD, is careful to place these sacrifices in the past ('for they used to...'), having just said that 'The Romans have put an end to their sacrificial and divinatory practices', but this could allow that the practices were still live when Caesar was in Gaul half a century earlier.

It is worth emphasizing that the texts at no time implicate the Druids with the act of sacrifice and augury – those were the functions of the Vates. The Druids, however, were present at these ceremonies. Diodorus says that no-one would make a sacrifice without a Druid being present, and Caesar confirms this by saying, 'the Druids officiate at such sacrifices'. This may seem like splitting hairs, but the issue is of particular interest in showing the sophisticated nature of Celtic ritual and belief systems, their practices separated between different participants with their own specific skill sets. This does not, however, mean that the Druids were innocent, even unwilling, bystanders at the gory sacrifices. They were an essential part of the process and were thus complicit.

The Posidonian tradition provides other details of Celtic beliefs and practices. Strabo records the practice of head-hunting, describing how when they leave the battlefield they attach the heads of their enemies to the necks of their horses, and when they reach home they nail the heads to the doors of their houses. He goes on to say:

> Posidonius says that he saw this sight in many places and was
> at first disquieted by it, but afterwards, becoming used to it,
> could bear it with equanimity. But they embalmed the heads of
> distinguished enemies with cedar-oil and used to make a display of
> them to strangers and were unwilling to let them be redeemed even
> for their weight in gold.

> (*Geog.* IV, IV, 4)

Exactly the same story is given by Diodorus, though without quoting his source. There is every reason to accept this account as an accurate description of Celtic behaviour in the 2nd and 1st centuries BC. The native temple sites in southern Gaul provide direct evidence of the central position played by the cult of the severed head, and isolated human skulls are found in archaeological contexts throughout Gaul and Britain. This was another practice to which the Romans put an end.

The information provided about sacred sites is rather more anecdotal. Diodorus reports that 'the Celts of the hinterland' have, what is to him, 'a strange and peculiar custom' with regard to religious loci:

> for in the temples and sanctuaries which are dedicated throughout the country a large amount of gold is openly placed as a dedication to the gods, and of the natives none touch it because of religious veneration.
>
> *(Hist. V, 26, 4)*

Much the same point is made, though obliquely, by Strabo, in his reference to lakes – presumably sacred lakes – in which they deposited quantities of silver and gold. He continues:

> In Tolosa, moreover, the temple was ... greatly esteemed by local inhabitants and for this reason the treasure there was unusually large since many made dedications and none would profane them.
>
> *(Geog. IV, I, 13)*

Strabo also refers to sacred islands. One, off the mouth of the Loire, is populated only by women who 'are possessed by Dionysus'. There were no men on the island, but the women were allowed to sail to the mainland for sexual gratification. Once a year they took the roof off their temple and re-roofed it within the day. All the women carried roofing material but one was deliberately nudged so that she dropped the load. She was immediately torn to pieces by the others, who paraded with the body parts around the temple, 'crying out "euoi" and do not cease until their madness passes'. He also quotes a 2nd-century BC geographer, Artemidorus, who tells of 'an island beside Britain in which sacrifices are performed like those performed in Samothrace in honour of Demeter and Core'. This is rather obscure but may suggest some kind of rite associated with the fertility of seed corn. It is interesting to wonder how Artemidorus came by this story – the most likely source would be Pytheas. Finally, another sacred island – the island of Sena, 'in the British Sea facing the shore of the Ossimians' – is mentioned by a 1st-century AD writer, Pomponius Mela, as the home of an oracle. The recurrence of sacred islands off the Atlantic coast is a reminder that the supernatural power of the sea must have featured large in the Celtic belief system. Islands, and perhaps promontories, would have been thought of as liminal places between land and ocean and as such charged with power.

The Posidonian tradition presents a coherent picture of the ritual and religious world of the Celts in which the Druids played an essential part as wise philosophers, revered for their justice, the keepers of natural and celestial knowledge, and the intermediaries between the gods and humankind. They were essentially specialists in a far more widespread system of beliefs and practices which involved other specialists – the Vates, who conducted the sacrifices and foretold the future; and the Bards, whose power lay in strengthening individuals through eulogy and destroying others through satire. Through the eyes of Posidonius we glimpse the system in all its complexities, but already the heavy hand of Rome was beginning to curtail those practices of which they purported to disapprove. Yet there is comparatively little censure in what Posidonius had to communicate – as he says himself, at first sight he was alarmed at some of what he saw but soon learned to be tolerant, as any good ethnographer should. His account gives us a rare insight into barbarian religious behaviour in the brief moment before Romanization caused irreparable change. All subsequent accounts reflect a disintegrating system viewed through a filter of Roman disapproval.

One incident provides a link between the old and the new. In the 60s of the 1st century BC, a German tribe, the Suebi, intent on moving into Gaulish territory, had encouraged the Gaulish

Sequani to take up arms against their neighbours, the Aedui – a tribe who had been traditionally friendly to Rome. About 60 BC, the tribe sent their chief magistrate, Divitiacus, who was a Druid, to Rome to seek help, and tradition has it that he addressed the Senate though to no good effect. Whilst in Rome he met Cicero and probably Caesar, who subsequently came to regard him as a friend. Cicero briefly mentions the meeting, noting that Divitiacus 'declared that he was acquainted with the system of nature which the Greeks call natural philosophy and he used to predict the future both by augury and inference'. The use of the past tense is interesting in that it implies that the role of Druids was changing and also perhaps that there may have been some blurring of functions between Druids and Vates. Divitiacus' return home was followed two years later by the first campaign in Caesar's war against the Gauls.

At the time of Divitiacus' visit to Rome, Julius Caesar's career was reaching a point of no return. Heavily in debt and confronted by powerful enemies, he desperately needed an opportunity to make a fast fortune and to establish a loyal military following. Both could be accomplished with a provincial command that offered the possibility of wars of conquest, and in 59 BC, as consul, he managed to engineer just such a command – the governorship of Cisalpine Gaul and Illyricum – which, by a special law, he was given for the exceptional period of five years. From this power base he could legitimately move against the Gauls or the Dacians under the guise of protecting the interests of Rome. After the Senate had agreed to add the province of Transalpine Gaul to his brief, he chose Free Gaul as the focus of his aggressive attentions, claiming that the routes to Spain had to be protected from disruption caused by unstable Gaulish tribes around the borders and that the movement of the German Suebi was a threat to Rome. To stir the deep-seated fear of barbarian attack from the north, ever present in the Roman mind, he claimed that if nothing was done about it, Gaul would be overrun by Germans.

In 58 BC, he moved first against the Helvetii, who were intent on migrating across the centre of Gaul, and in the autumn against the German Suebi. The conquest had begun. It took eight years of intensive campaigning before the exhausted Gaulish resistance petered out. The huge territory from the Pyrenees to the Rhine was now, at least notionally, under the command of Rome and the process of Romanization could begin. In fact, in the decades immediately following the cessation of the war progress was slow and not least because Rome was now caught up in a vicious civil war, but eventually, in 12 BC, with the dedication of the altar to Rome and Augustus at Lugdunum (Lyon), the initial stage of colonization was complete and the new provinces could begin to take their place in the fast-expanding Roman Empire. In eight years of conquest, during which, if we are to believe one near-contemporary commentator, one-third of the Gaulish population was killed and another third sold into slavery, the social and belief systems of Free Gaul were shattered. It took a whole generation and more before the traumas of war faded and a new social order emerged, neither Gaulish nor Roman but Gallo-Roman.

Eight years of relentless campaigning cannot have failed to have taught Caesar much about Gaulish society and yet, in his *Commentaries on the Gallic War*, he tells us surprisingly little, largely because his theme is a campaign narrative and his intent to glorify his own achievements. There are, however, many small details to be gleaned from his elegantly efficient prose and at one point, in Book VI dealing with the events in the year 53 BC, he breaks off to give a succinct ethnographic account of the customs of the Gauls and Germans, much as would have been expected by his readers. It is quite possible that this section was added to the *Commentaries* at a later stage when he was editing the work for public consumption. It reads quite differently from the rest and suggests that he may have been consulting texts as he wrote. One of those texts may well have been Posidonius, but if so Caesar was no straight copyist.

Unlike the Posidonian tradition, Caesar does not divide the class of wise men into functional categories: to him, there are only two privileged classes in Celtic society, the Knights and the Druids. Either this can be taken as an oversimplification of the complex ritual system, done deliberately or through ignorance, or it reflects a change that had taken place, with the difference in activities of the Druids and Vates now being obscured in practice. Some have argued that Caesar wanted to present the Druids as dangerous extremists, and thus it was in the interests of effective propaganda to give the impression that they were directly responsible for human sacrifice. This may be so, but it could equally be that Caesar was not concerned with the niceties and simply wanted to give a quick overall impression of Celtic religion.

He begins with a succinct summary:

Druids

> The Druids are in charge of religion. They have control over public and private sacrifices, and give rulings on all religious questions. Large numbers of young men go to them for instruction, and they are greatly honoured by the people.

and then proceeds to the detail. He repeats what many writers had said before, that the Druids believed that souls did not perish but passed from one body to another, they:

> hold long discussions about the heavenly bodies and their movements, about the size of the universe and the earth, about the nature of the physical world and about the power and properties of the immortal gods.

and they 'officiate at sacrifices'. There is nothing new in any of this; it is dealt with briefly but there are three themes which he warms to and which probably derive from his own observations.

The first is the power the Druids had over society:

In almost all disputes, between communities or between individuals the Druids act as judges. If a crime is committed, if there is a murder, or if there is a dispute about inheritance or a boundary they are the ones who give a verdict and decide on the punishment or compensation appropriate in each case. Any individual or community not abiding by their verdict is banned from the sacrifice and this is regarded among the Gauls as the most severe punishment. Those who are banned ... are reckoned as sacrilegious criminals. Everyone shuns them; no-one will go near or speak to them for fear of being contaminated in some way ... If they make any petitions there is no justice for them, and they are excluded from any position of importance.

(*BG* VI, 13)

Although other sources have mentioned the judicial power of Druids, the details which Caesar gives are new and the rather laborious way he makes the point suggests that he was impressed (or he wanted his audience to be) about the near-absolute power that the Druids wielded in society. They controlled the lives of all men.

His second concern builds on this: they were teachers with an eager following. He repeats the point three times. In his Introduction, he says 'Large numbers of young men go to them for instruction'. Writing of their knowledge of the heavens, he adds that in these subjects, 'they also give instruction to their pupils'; and later he expands further:

The Druids are exempt from military service and do not pay taxes like the rest. Such significant privileges attract many students, some of whom come of their own accord to be taught while others are sent by priests and relatives.

During their training, he says, they had to learn a great many verses by heart and some people spend as long as 20 years learning the doctrine. The implication here seems to be that a

8. 'An Archdruid in his Judicial Habit'. The aquatint by S. R. Meyrick and C. H. Smith, published in 1815, was a work of fiction but incorporated depictions of real artefacts of differing dates. It was influential in creating the vision of the Druid popular in the public imagination from the 19th century to the present time

distinction can be made between the general teaching of a large number of the young and the specific, more intensive training needed to become a master of the discipline. Caesar seems not to understand the importance of oral learning among 'barbarian' societies, but instead tries to explain it away by suggesting that they do it deliberately to improve the memory and to keep the knowledge inaccessible. By building up the idea of exclusivity and the extent of the influence which the Druids had over the young, Caesar is again stressing their power.

Finally, he comes more closely to his main concern – the ability of the Druids to exercise their control across tribal boundaries: they are, he tells us, a pan-national brotherhood ruled by an archdruid with supreme authority over the rest. Succession is through distinction, but if there are several contenders the matter is put to the vote, 'though sometimes they even fight to decide who will be their leader'. They also held an annual gathering on a fixed date at a consecrated place in the territory of the Carnutes which they believed to be the centre of Gaul. 'People who have disputes to settle assemble there from all over the country and accept the rulings and judgements of the Druids.' Such an annual meeting would have presented a potential danger for Rome: they were occasions when anti-Roman attitudes could be aired and the injustices of the occupying forces examined in public. It was well within the power of the presiding Druids to manipulate sentiment and call for unified action. It may be no coincidence that when rebellion came in the spring of 52 BC it began in the territory of the Carnutes, though Caesar makes no mention of Druid involvement.

The annual assembly of the Druids was probably deeply rooted in society, and as Gaul became increasingly Romanized, the need to control it became pressing. The ingenious solution came when, in 12 BC, the Emperor Augustus' stepson Drusus dedicated an altar to Rome and Augustus at a sanctuary on an island at the confluence of the rivers Rhône and Saône at Lugdunum (Lyon) and proclaimed that here the newly created *concilium Galliarum* (Council of the Gauls) would meet annually on 1 August – the midsummer Celtic festival of Lugnasad. It was a clever solution, bringing the national assembly under Roman auspices. The date chosen was, by coincidence, the birthday of the emperor.

In selecting what he had to say of the Druids, Caesar was intent to emphasize the very considerable power he believed they held over Gaulish society. While his emphasis may have been deliberate, to provide some justification for his repressive treatment of the Gauls, there is no reason to suppose that he was in any way falsifying the evidence. His account can be accepted as an assessment of the situation as he observed it in the 50s of the 1st century BC.

Caesar has more to say about the religion of the Gauls, though he separates this from his main description of the Druids. The Gauls, he said, were very superstitious; 'consequently people suffering from serious illness, and people involved in the dangers of battle, make, or promise to make, human sacrifice'. He adds that Druids officiate at such sacrifices, echoing the Posidonian tradition that for a sacrifice to be valid, a Druid had to be present to serve as an intermediary with the gods. Caesar then warms to his theme: 'The Gauls believe the power of the immortal gods can be appeased only if one human life is exchanged for another, and they have sacrifices of this kind regularly established by the community.' Then follows a description of the familiar wicker man ritual. While this kind of thing may have been going on in the more remote parts of Gaul through which Caesar had campaigned, the close similarity to the Posidonian text suggests that Caesar may have been importing this colourful description from an earlier source. Perhaps his motive was, as some have suggested, to horrify his readers and to justify his own acts of repression, yet he offers his descriptions of Gaulish sacrifices as crisp reportage devoid of any trace of moral judgement.

There is no doubt that Roman administrators would have found human sacrifice to be an unacceptable practice. Strabo, quoting Posidonius (referring to the Gauls of the province of Transalpina), says as much: 'The Romans have put an end to this behaviour (head-hunting) and also to their sacrificial and divinatory practices opposed to our customs.' Caesar would have extended these prohibitions to the rest of Gaul. Pomponius Mela, a mid-1st-century AD writer, provides a little more detail:

There still remain traces of atrocious customs no longer practised, and although they now refrain from outright slaughter yet they still draw blood from the victims led to the altar.

(*De Situ Orbis* III, 2, 18)

Since the rest of his texts simply recycle scraps gleaned from earlier accounts, most notably Caesar's, it is quite likely that this detail of surrogate sacrifice reflects the situation at or soon after the time of the Gallic Wars.

Pomponius Mela was writing in the censorious age of the Early Empire when public figures could show shock and horror at the behaviour of the barbarians they had newly conquered: his phrase 'atrocious customs' would have struck a chord with his readers. The 1st century AD was a time of official repression. Pliny tells us that 'magic' still flourished in Gaul into the time of his own memory, but the Emperor Tiberius had issued a decree against 'the Druids and the whole tribe of diviners and physicians' – an interesting statement that still makes the distinction between Druids and Vates. Another writer, Suetonius, in his *Life* of Claudius, records that the emperor:

very thoroughly suppressed the barbarous and inhuman religion of the Druids in Gaul, which in the time of Augustus had merely been forbidden to Roman citizens.

(*Claudius* 25)

Taken together, these texts leave little doubt that, in the first half of the 1st century AD, the Roman authorities made sustained efforts to break the power of the Druids. The 'savage rites' long since suppressed, the Druids still remained a threat to the state by virtue of their unifying powers over the people. It is quite possible that Druids were involved in fermenting the rebellion that broke out in Gaul in AD 21 led by Florus and Sacrovir, and the later revolt of AD 68 initiated by Vindex – the Gaulish-born governor of the province of Lugdunensis. There is no direct evidence that this was so, but both rebellions began with the Gaulish elite assembling and deciding to go to war. In a telling aside, the historian Tacitus, writing of the fire that destroyed the Roman Capitol in AD 70, adds that 'The Druids declared, with the prophetic utterance of an idle superstition that [the fire] was a sign of the anger of heaven' and that it portended the rise of the Gaulish nations. Clearly the Druids were still an articulate force. When Pliny later wrote that 'we cannot too highly appreciate our debt to the Romans for having put an end to this monstrous cult', he was thinking more of the stability of the empire than the letting of a little barbarian blood.

The last great set piece description of Druids in action is Tacitus' description of events in Britain in AD 59/60 when the Roman army campaigning in north Wales approached the island of Anglesey, where the British opposition forces had assembled:

> ... between the ranks dashed women dressed in black like the Furies, with hair dishevelled, waving torches. All around, the Druids lifting up their hands to heaven and pouring forth dreadful imprecations scared our soldiers by the unfamiliar sight so that, as if their limbs were paralyzed they stood motionless and exposed to wounds.

Eventually Roman discipline prevails, as is usual in these set piece battle accounts, the opposition was routed and:

> Their groves, devoted to inhuman superstition, were destroyed. They [the Druids] decreed it a duty to cover their altars with the blood of captives and to consult their deities through human entrails.

> (*Annals* XIV, 30)

There is no reason to doubt that Druids were present at the engagement on Anglesey, and the presence of women is an interesting detail, but the blood and entrails sound rather like an author spicing up his tale by stirring in some old familiar prejudices. Yet it is possible that in a remote island like Britain traditional rituals were still practised in time of great stress. Pliny may have been mindful of this even when he wrote that in Britannia the fascination with magic still remained and rites were performed with much ceremony.

The emotive anti-Druid language of the 1st century AD is redolent of Rome's intention to stamp out traditional belief systems and behaviour. But there is something more to it – the desire to conjure up in the mind of the reader a vision of barbarous times past and to induce a *frisson* of fear. Nowhere is the literary 'topos' of 'barbarous religion' better evoked than in a poem, *Pharsalia*, written by Lucan in the middle of the 1st century AD.

A grove there was, untouched by men's hands from ancient times, whose interlacing boughs enclosed a space of darkness and cold shade, and banished the sunlight far above. No rural Pan dwelt there, no Silvanus, ruler of the woods, no Nymphs; but gods were worshipped there with savage rites, the altars were heaped with hideous offerings, and every tree was sprinkled with human gore. On those boughs...birds feared to perch; in those coverts wild beasts would not lie down; no wind ever bore down upon that wood, nor thunderbolt hurled from black clouds; the trees, even when they spread their leaves to no breeze, rustled of themselves. Water, also, fell there in abundance from dark springs. The images of the gods, grim and rude, were uncouth blocks formed of felled tree-trunks. Their mere antiquity and the ghastly hue of their rotten timber struck terror....Legend also told that often the subterranean hollows quaked and bellowed, that yew-trees fell down and rose again, that the glare of conflagration came from trees that were not on fire, and that serpents twined and glided round the stems. The people never resorted thither to worship at close quarters, but left the place to the gods.

Poetic licence no doubt, but effective nonetheless.

After the flurry of writing on the Druids in the 1st century AD, the record becomes almost silent, though there are a few whispers. In 3rd-century Gaul, the prophecies of Druidesses (*dryades*) are mentioned on three separate occasions, though in contexts which imply that they were nothing more than lone fortune tellers. It is possible that the word 'Druid' was now being used quite unspecifically to refer to any being claiming supernatural powers.

There is, however, some hint that the memory of the Druids of the past was still alive in late Roman Gaul. Ausonius mentions them in two passages. In one, he recalls the tradition that a friend was descended from the Druids of Bayeux, associated with the temple of Belenus, and in another he mentions a man, who was rumoured to have been descended from the Druids of Armorica, becoming a teacher in the university of Bordeaux. In neither case should we put too much store on these remarks – both were based on hearsay – but what is interesting is that now, in the late 4th century, a Druid was considered to be an acceptable ancestor.

Chapter 6
Twilight in the far west

Julius Caesar mounted two expeditions to Britain in 55 and 54 BC but tells us little of the people he encountered except to stress their general similarity to the Gauls. He did, however, offer the tantalizing observation that it was believed that the doctrine of the Druids was developed in Britain and that 'even today those who want to study the doctrine in greater detail usually go to Britain to learn there'. His two brief campaigns brought the south-east of Britain close to the Roman world. Trade flourished and people moved with comparative ease between Britain and the Continent for the next 90 years or so until, in AD 43, the Emperor Claudius decided to annex the island and make it a province of Rome. As we have seen, in the course of the conquest the Roman army had at least one engagement that involved Druids when they attacked the island of Anglesey off the north-west coast of Wales in AD 59/60.

Although the armies, under the governor Agricola, penetrated deep into the Highlands of Scotland, and even visited Orkney when circumnavigating the extremities of the island, by the end of the 1st century AD the frontier had been established on a line between the River Tyne and the Solway estuary – a line later taken by Hadrian's Wall. During the 2nd century, a new frontier, the Antonine Wall, was created to the north between the Forth and the Clyde, but occupation was brief and the more southern frontier became the established limit of empire. Though the Highlands of Scotland, the Northern and Western Isles, and Ireland lay outside the Roman domain, these regions were within comparatively easy reach of traders.

Throughout prehistory, Ireland played an integral part in the maritime exchange networks which bound the Atlantic-facing lands of Europe together, but after the middle of the 1st millennium BC trade slackened and Ireland began to be increasingly isolated. It was not until the 1st century BC that contacts across the Irish Sea, between Britain and Ireland, picked up again.

Caesar says nothing of Ireland, and Strabo, writing in the early decades of the 1st century AD, had little to report other than the rumour that its inhabitants were more savage than the Britons and indulged in incest and cannibalism. Where Strabo picked up this hearsay is unclear, unless it was something gleaned from Pytheas, who had journeyed the length of the Irish Sea, probably stopping at the Isle of Man on his circumnavigation of Britain in the 4th century BC. Forty years after the invasion of Britain, Tacitus had access to far more information. He tells us that through the activities of merchants the harbours of Ireland were reasonably well known and the land and people of Ireland were not unlike Britain and the British. Information continued to accumulate and by the end of the 2nd century AD, the astronomer Ptolemy was able to give latitude and longitude coordinates of 55 locations, many of them coastal features but also of tribes and major settlements. The distribution of Roman artefacts shows that the parts of Ireland most heavily affected by trade were the east and north coasts facing Britain. One of the principal ports-of-trade was established on the coastal promontory of Drumanagh, a few kilometres north of the mouth of the Liffey.

By the 4th century, the dynamics of contact had changed. Some Irishmen were now employed as mercenaries in the Roman army, while others indulged in piracy and raiding against western parts of Britain. The story told in the *Confessio* of St Patrick throws some light on the situation in the early 5th century. As a boy, Patrick was brought up in Britain but was captured by an Irish raiding party and taken off to Ireland to serve as a slave looking after flocks and herds. He eventually escaped on a ship which was transporting Irish hunting dogs, probably to Gaul, and eventually made his way back to Britain. These were troubled times when the old Roman order was breaking down and there was mobility at all levels, including the settlement of Irish communities in Wales, Scotland, and possibly in Cornwall.

In 431, so a later chronicler records, the pope sent a Gaulish churchman, Palladius, to minister to the Irish. There is some place-name evidence to suggest that he was active for a while in south-west Wales before taking ship to Ireland to begin his mission in Co. Wicklow, but little seems to have followed from it. The next year Patrick sailed back to Ireland from Britain and, basing himself on Armagh in the north, set out on a far more successful mission. He travelled extensively, baptizing people and ordaining clergy and establishing a system of *parochia* – rural territories focused around a church.

At the same time, in the middle of the 5th century, another Christian movement – monasticism – was beginning to gain hold in Ireland, spreading from the Mediterranean region along the Atlantic seaways. It proved to be extremely popular, and by the 6th century was beginning to replace the system of *parochia* set up by Patrick. Gradually, the power of bishops waned, and by the end of the century a system of independent monastic communities, living by the rule of their founders, had spread throughout Ireland and to many parts of western and northern Britain. The new monasteries were centres of scholarship and of teaching and, with proselytizing zeal, they set about replacing the pagan beliefs and culture of the countryside with their own distinctive form of Christianity.

It was in the monasteries that the rich oral culture of pagan Ireland was transcribed, edited, and copied. One scribe, in a marginal note, was honest enough to admit that he did not really understand what he was copying, but the original transcribers had their own agendas. They were careful how they presented the beliefs and values of the pagan culture they were trying to educate. Schooled in the Classics and with an intimate knowledge of the Bible, it was only natural that they sought to make connections by identifying universal truths in the ancient sagas they were committing to script. That said, the vernacular literature, as it survives for us to read today, still contains much that echoes pre-Christian beliefs and behaviour.

If the sagas and hero tales reflect, albeit in emasculated form, a glimpse of pre-Christian times, the Law Tracts, originating in the 7th and 8th centuries, and the *Lives* of the saints and the hymns, composed and written down in succeeding centuries, inform us more directly of the social structures and values of early Christian Ireland. By comparing the two sources, it is possible to chart the rapid decline in the power and prestige of the Druids as Christianity makes its inexorable inroads.

What, then, can we learn of pagan beliefs in pre-Christian Ireland? To begin with, the gods were many and everywhere, much as they were in pre-Roman Gaul. In former times, it was believed, they were controlled by the Tribes of the Goddess Dana, but later they comprised a loose web of supernatural beings usually inhabiting the underground regions but entering the realms of the humans from time to time. They had many attributes and were visualized in many forms, but these different manifestations could be reduced to two powers, one male, the other female, whose balanced opposition created a state of unstable equilibrium.

The female power was a goddess of the earth and of water – springs and rivers and lakes. She was a mother goddess controlling fertility and productivity, providing nourishment for the people and presiding over the seasons and the seasonal feasts: her very abundance was sometimes expressed by her triple form. But she also had within her the power of destruction and the fury of slaughter – the opposites of nurture and fertility – and could bring devastation and death. In this dangerously unstable form she appears in the tales as the ferocious Morrígan, who needed careful handling and much propitiation.

The male god was the Dagda – the good god, in the sense of being good at everything. He was the father of the tribe and could appear in the guise of a craftsman, a warrior, or a being with magical powers. His feasting was voracious, as was his sexual appetite, reflecting both his virility and his command of plenty. The Dagda engaged in intercourse with the Morrígan once a year on the feast of Samain, thus commanding her protection for his people for the year to come.

There is something satisfyingly simple in the neat binary opposition of the Dagda and the Morrígan, even though they do appear in a confusion of different guises. There is, however, another male deity – Lug – who at first sight seems to stand aside as something different. He is the antithesis of the Dagda – young, beautiful, and pure, contrasting with the aged, ugly, grossness of the Dagda. His weapons are throwing weapons – the sling and the spear – very different to the Dagda's heavy club, and whereas the Dagda commands all knowledge, Lug is the many-skilled. One way to structure this would be to see the Lug/Dagda dichotomy as the two opposing sides of a single male deity, much as the Morrígan encompasses the oppositions of wellbeing and destruction contained within the female form. In the overarching scheme, then, the productive and destructive forces of nature confront the traditional and progressive forces in humanity.

Another aspect of religious life that is readily apparent in the vernacular literature is the passage of time. The year is divided into two halves: the light half, which begins with the festival of Beltane (1 May) and ends with the ceremony of Samain (1 November); and the dark half, which runs from Samain to Beltane. The two halves are themselves divided into two by the ceremonies of Imbolc (1 February) and Lugnasad (1 August). As we have seen, there are reflections of this division in the Coligny calendar, suggesting that the scheme was widely adopted throughout the Celtic world.

The seasonal divide was highly relevant to an agricultural community totally dependent on efficient grain production and the wellbeing of its flocks and herds. The first quarter of the year from Samain to Imbolc was a quiet time when the natural world was dormant, but Imbolc (1 February) saw the beginnings of new life with the start of the lambing season and the lactation of ewes. With the beginning of summer at Beltane (1 May), the livestock had to be moved out on to the upland pasture and as a prelude cattle were driven between two fires to purify them from the diseases incubated during their winter confinement. Lugnasad (1 August) was the central point of the harvest celebrations when the grain was brought in for safe storage. It was also a time for large social gatherings where the business of the tribe could be transacted, legal agreements entered into, and marriages arranged. Now the propitiatory offerings to the gods had to be made in thanks for the success of the harvest and in preparation for the long liminal period of winter. As we have seen, Lugnasad was chosen by the Roman authorities in Gaul as the appropriate time for the meeting of the *concilium Galliarum*. Finally the year ended with Samain (1 November). This was the time when the livestock were brought in from the open pastures and the beasts not chosen for overwintering were killed and their meat preserved: it was a time of feasting before the privations of winter took hold.

Samain was also the end of one year and the beginning of the next. It was a liminal time and as such was dangerous. It was now

Druids

that the union between the Dagda and the Morrígan took place – an act symbolizing the taming of the wilder powers of nature. But in the brief gap between year end and year beginning – the night of 31 October and 1 November – chaos could reign as the spirits and deities of the nether-world below swarmed into the world of humans.

In an attempt to contain these beliefs and superstitions, the Christians took over the ceremonies of 1 November and made it All Saints Day in the Christian calendar, but the night before – Halloween – still retains a strong flavour of the pagan past, even today, in its contemporary guises, traditional and invented. The festival of Imbolc was also subsumed into the Christian calendar as the Saint's Day of St Brigit, herself a reflection of a pagan Irish goddess, while Beltane is still celebrated widely throughout Europe in the many different manifestations of May Day.

In pre-Christian and early Christian times, Ireland was divided into perhaps as many as 150 tribes (*túatha*), each ruled by a king. Some of the kings would have been more powerful than others and able to command the allegiances of lesser kings. The king was all powerful within his *túath*. He would, by right, expect the loyalty of all his free men and could summon them to form a military force in the event of a threat or when a raid was being planned. He would also preside at the *óenach* – a regular assembly at which the business of the *túath* was considered and decided upon.

Irish society was highly hierarchical, the many ranks being carefully circumscribed and their powers and privileges defined in the Law Tracts. Broadly speaking, there were two principal divisions, the free (*sóer*) and the unfree (*dóer*), and among the free there was a specially privileged class, the *nemed*, which included the king, the lord, the cleric, and the poet. Since *nemed* is cognate with *nemeton*, which means 'sacred place', it suggests that the privileged class were at one time embraced within the religious system. One early medieval Law Tract states that the *túath*, to be worthy of the title, had to have a king, an ecclesiastical scholar, a churchman, and a poet. This was long after Ireland had been Christianized, but the structure clearly reflects that of pagan times when the king was regarded as semi-divine and was supported by a religious philosopher (*drui*), a seer (*fili*), and a poet (*bard*) – a system closely reflecting the Druids, Vates, and Bards of the pre-Roman Gauls.

The *druid*, *filid*, and *baird* performed the functions expected of the privileged class. Already, in 2nd-century BC Gaul, it was possible to detect the blurring of functions between the Vates and the Druids, and this conflation is evident in pre-Christian Ireland. The Druids were still the most powerful of the wise men: they were the mediators between the deities and humans, the arbitrators in disputes, and, since they could foretell the future, their skills were in demand by kings preparing to embark on new pursuits. Perhaps more important, the Druids were involved in setting the prohibitions (*geasa*) which controlled the freedoms of the king. A *geis* was an imperative of magical character which circumscribed behaviour, for example the prohibition on eating horse flesh before mounting a chariot or of straightening your spear point with your teeth. The more sacred power a king had, the greater were his *geasa*: breaking a single one could render even a great king powerless. There is one instance of a king whose *geis* forbade him to speak in company before his Druid had spoken. The story goes that the assembly remained in silence until the Druid asked the king what was the matter.

The *filidh* shared with the Druids the power of prophecy and divination, and as such they were in the confidence of the king, but they seem now to have acquired additional powers. They had become teachers (it could take up to 12 years' instruction to become proficient in the discipline) and they had also taken over some responsibility for poetry and satire from the bards. The bards remained but their tasks were restricted to composing eulogies and keeping alive the oral traditions of society through public storytelling. This shift in power was exacerbated as Christianity took hold. The Druids were soon suppressed and, by the 7th century, had ceased to be a distinct order, while the *filidh* had grown in strength and influence and were allowed to continue many of their old practices alongside, and in harmony with, the Church. They were still a distinct and powerful order up to the 17th century, when the bureaucracy of the English government finally saw to their demise.

The story of the Druids in Ireland is, therefore, one of decline. In the pre-Christian sagas we can see some of them still in action. One of the best known is Cathbad, who appears in the Ulster Cycle tale, the *Taín Bó Cuailnge*. Cathbad had spent his early life as the leader of an exterritorial war band (*fiana*) but had lately become the Druid of King Conchobar, who was quite possibly his foster son. Cathbad is seen offering prophecies – that he who took up arms on a particular day would achieve fame and greatness but his life would be short (it was the hero Cú Chulainn who met the challenge), and that a pregnant woman would give birth to a daughter called Deirdre who would bring Ulster to ruins (she did). Here is Cathbad the Druid as a seer able to divine the future. He is also portrayed as a teacher of the young who always had a hundred pupils about him learning the druidic discipline. Elsewhere, we see him in action trying, in vain, to protect Cú Chulainn from the magic of the warrior Queen Medb.

In other stories, Druids appear as the interpreters of dreams and as the mediators between the gods and the king. They are magicians able to conjure up storms to drive off invaders or, like the Black Druid, able to turn a young woman into a deer because she had refused his attentions. We learn little of the organization of the Druids from the Irish sources. Often they appear as lone individuals, but sometimes in groups, and it would seem that all Druids, and later the *filidh*, were overseen by one of their number elected for the purpose. In some traditions they were associated with Uisnech, the 'navel' of Ireland, where their assemblies were held. This has distinct similarities to the annual assemblies of the Gaulish Druids held in the centre of Gaul, in the territory of the Carnutes.

These anecdotal scraps, gleaned from the Irish vernacular literature, offer a glimpse of the Irish Druid, in the centuries before Christianity, as a man of power, established in the courts of kings, able to serve as an intermediary between the gods and men. But there is also a sense that they had now begun to take on the role of magicians and sorcerers. How much this reflects their changing role in society it is difficult to say, but it is as well to remember that we are seeing them through the eyes of the Christian scribes who transcribed and edited the stories and to whom the old order was anathema. Perhaps the Druid is now beginning to be written out of the story.

Conflict between druidism and Christianity was inevitable, but at first there are hints of some kind of stand-off. In the 7th-century text *Vita Brigitae*, describing the life of St Brigit a century or so before, Brigit's foster father is a Druid, entirely benign in all his actions though overawed by the power of the Church. Another document, of the 6th century, the *First Synod of St Patrick*, describes how oaths were sworn in the presence of a Druid, and in texts of about the same date we learn of the Druids' continued power in warfare. They are able to erect barriers (whether real or virtual is unclear) beyond which anyone who ventured would be killed, and a Druid still had the power to make the weaker side win. In these early encounters the Christians were treading carefully.

Yet the conflict between the two ideologies was real, and it was in the interests of Christians, who after all controlled the written word, to record it in such a way that Christianity was seen to have the more powerful magic. Thus when Patrick appeared in the court of King Leogarie to convert the king, the king's Druids put up a strong resistance. Patrick's response was to pray to his god for the death of one of the Druids, which subsequently happened. The contest continued at the great feast at Tara. Having successfully avoided poisoning, Patrick agreed to the king's suggestion of ordeal by fire involving the Druid Lucat and one of Patrick's followers, Benignus. Needless to say, the Christians won. What truth, if any, there is in these tales it is impossible to say. It is true that reductors were influenced by Old Testament stories but what is significant is that they choose to present the coming of Christianity in terms of a traditional conflict by magic and sorcery – the Christians are playing by pagan rules and winning. The symbolic culmination comes when Patrick lights a great fire on the Hill of Slane – a pagan sacred site – before a fire could be lit on the Hill of Tara. This was in direct defiance of pagan tradition and signifies the final ascendancy of the new religion.

By the time that the Law Tracts were being composed in the 7th and 8th centuries, it is clear that those Druids who had survived had been reduced to the level of the sorcerer and the quack. In one text, the status of the Druid, assessed in terms of entitlement to sick maintenance, is argued to be that of a *bóaire* (a freeman farmer), equivalent to a satirist and brigand. He is no longer among the *nemed* – the privileged class. Druids are now seen to be the makers of love-potions and the casters of spells but little else.

The *nemed* class, as we have seen, included the king, the lord, the cleric, and the poet. There was also a lower rank – *dóernemed* (base-*nemed*) – to which belonged physicians, judges, blacksmiths, coppersmiths, harpists, and carpenters. The Christian cleric now assumed the tasks once performed by the Druid. The Law texts make clear that the high-ranking clerics were equal to, or in some cases superior to, kings, and this is reflected in their honour prices. They were the philosophers and men of wisdom providing guidance and advice to the kings; they were the intermediaries between the new Christian god and the people; and it was they who taught the young.

9. The ritual complex at Tara, Co. Meath, Ireland. The site begins with a neolithic burial chamber and continues as a place of great religious importance into the early historic period

Next to the clerics were the poets (*filidh*), men who could affect the status of others through the power of their words. The similarity between the Gaulish Bards and Vates and the Irish *filidh* is striking and implies a strong thread of continuity in both social structure and practice. In Gaulish society, the Bards were singers and poets and could use their powers to demean a man through satire or boost his prowess through eulogy, while the Vates had powers of divination. The Irish *filidh* seem to have embraced the powers of both classes. They were certainly known for the power of their satire. Their words could raise blisters on the face of an opponent and even had the power to kill.

In the early 15th century, the death of the Lord Lieutenant was ascribed to a poet's spell, and as late as the 16th century it was believed that poets could 'rhyme to death' animals and men. The poet would also compose praise-poems and eulogies for his patrons and would expect to be rewarded accordingly. For a high-quality composition he might receive a chariot, and some poets could become as rich as even the king or the Church. This is reflected in the story told by Posidonius of the Gaulish King Louernius who, in the late 2nd century BC, organized a massive feast to boost his status. The Bard arrived too late for the festivities but being quick-witted

> ... composed a song magnifying [the king's] greatness and lamenting his own late arrival. Louernius was very pleased and asked for a bag of gold and threw it to the poet who ran beside his chariot. The poet picked it up and sang another song saying that the very tracks made by his chariot in the earth gave gold and largesse to mankind.

> (*Athenaeus* IV, 37)

In addition to these traditional skills, the Irish *filidh* had now acquired the powers of prophecy. He was also a storyteller and a person who retained in his memory the history, genealogy, and lore of his people. A poet of the top grade was expected to know 350 stories. This knowledge poets learned in schools run by qualified *fili* which they attended for between 7 and 12 years. They were also involved in both the theory and practice of the law. One story tells of a *fili* who had been converted to Christianity, discussing the Laws with St Patrick. That which was not in conflict with Christianity was retained to form the basis of the legal systems 'of the judges of the Church and the poets'. Another text mentions the poet's entitlement to fees for his knowledge of different forms of judgment.

It is clear that the *filidh* had now taken on a range of tasks that had previously been in the purview of the Druids, and the class had become correspondingly more complex with many different grades matching ability, length of training, and range of activity. There were two broad categories – the *fili*, who were of the higher rank, and the *bards*, who were less accomplished. The *fili* were divided into 7 grades, while there were 16 grades of *bard*. This broad twofold divide between *fili* and *bards* may be a reflection of the divide apparent in Gaul between the Vates and the Bards, but in the more evolved Irish system the powers of the two had been brought together, augmented by some of the functions of the Druids as druidism was suppressed to the extent of extinction, and redistributed in a more rigorous class system.

In Ireland, the *filidh* continued to perform the tasks of poets, advisers, lawyers, teachers, and seers to as late as the 17th century, when their functions lapsed under English rule and the order wasted away. But still there remained the fear of poet as satirist. One 20th-century poet, Tomás O Criomhthainn, describes how he was prepared to spend a day listening to an island poet (*fili*) lest he suffered being satirized!

The imposition of Christianity on Irish society and the suppression of native paganism took centuries to become effective. This is no better illustrated than in the story told by Giraldus Cambrensis in his *Description of Ireland*, written about 1185, about the inauguration of the king of an Ulster clan:

> The whole people of that country being gathered in one place, a white mare is led into the midst of them, and he who is to be inaugurated, not as a prince but as a brute, not as a king but as an outlaw, comes before the people on all fours, confessing himself a beast with no less impudence than imprudence. The mare being immediately killed, and cut in pieces and boiled, a bath is prepared for him from the broth. Sitting in this he eats the flesh which is brought to him, the people standing round and partaking also.

He is also required to drink the broth in which he is bathed, not drawing it in any vessel, nor even in his hand, but lapping it with his mouth. These unrighteous rites being duly accomplished, his royal authority and dominion are ratified.

(*Topographia Hibernica*, iii, 25)

To Giraldus, it 'was barbarous and abominable', but what he was reporting was an ancient rite of kingship requiring the king-to-be to have intercourse (simulated or real) with the mother goddess in the form of a mare. By this union and the consumption of her flesh, the king was uniting his tribe with the powers of nature, thus ensuring their wellbeing. That the ceremony was still being performed in the 12th century is a remarkable example of pagan survival.

Chapter 7
Renaissance and rediscovery

It is a deep-seated need of human societies to understand their origins. Nowadays we can build models of increasing complexity on the basis of DNA studies and archaeological research, but before the 19th century there was little tangible evidence to rely on other than the Bible and a few Classical texts. A medieval chronicler intent on creating a foundation myth had two broad choices, either he could begin with the sons of Noah colonizing the earth in the aftermath of the Flood or he could extend the highly respectable myth of Rome's origins founded, so Livy believed, by Aeneas fleeing from the flames of Troy. Thus, in France in the 7th century, the Franks were said to be the successors of King Francio who had journeyed west after the fall of Troy. But in another story the founder was Francus, who was descended from Japhet, son of Noah, who colonized Europe after the Flood. Francus, so the story goes, was one of four brothers, the others being Romanus, founder of the Gallo-Romans; Britto, who established the Bretons; and Albanus, the father of the Alamanni. The 9th-century British chronicler Nennius warmed to the story but corrected it, arguing that Britto had in fact founded the Britons. And so the confection grew.

It was the publication of Geoffrey of Monmouth's great work *Historia Regum Britanniae* around 1135 that produced the first fully fledged myth of British origins. Geoffrey was a Welsh cleric, probably based in Oxford, who claimed to have had access to a very old Breton manuscript which provided his source material. But there are clear indications that this was not so and that the early 'history' was a creation of Geoffrey's imaginative mind. Geoffrey's story is simple: the history of Britain begins with Brutus, a Trojan warrior who, around 1170 BC, landed at Totnes and overcame the Giants who were already occupying the island. He went on to found New Troy (London) and was succeeded by his sons, who became the kings of England, Scotland, and Wales. Thereafter the succession of kings, including Lud, Cole, Vortigern, and Arthur, was detailed to link up to the early Saxon king lists, thus providing Britain with a satisfyingly continuous history. Geoffrey had produced a compelling story which achieved great popularity in the medieval world and grew richer and more intricate through many elaborations and accretions. Although by the 17th century doubts were being expressed, Geoffrey's stories proved to be remarkably resilient and in some quarters were still being repeated as reliable history into the 19th century.

The Biblical model, based on the Old Testament stories of the Flood and its aftermath, provided a strong underpinning for 16th- and 17th-century narrative histories like the *Rerum Scoticarum Historia* of George Buchanan (1506–82), *Britannia Antiqua Illustrata* by Aylett Sammes (c. 1636–c. 1679), and *Antiquité de la nation et de la langue des Celts* by the Breton theologian Paul-Yves Pezron (1639–1706). Pezron's book, published in French in 1703 and in English in 1706, was particularly influential in the development of ideas about the Celts. He believed that they were descended from Gomer, grandson of Noah, and spread across Europe from the east, eventually settling in Brittany and Wales. His work was widely read and brought the notion of the Celts, as ancestors, to the attention of the world of scholarship.

Antiquarians writing in the 16th century and later had far more source material to use than their medieval predecessors. With the opening up of monastic libraries, the manuscript texts of Classical writers were beginning to become more widely known, and it was from the works of Caesar, Tacitus, and Pliny that knowledge of the Celts (or Gauls) and the Druids came more firmly into the public consciousness. The printing press hastened the dissemination of these works. The *Gallic Wars* was printed in Latin in 1511, making Caesar's famous account of Celtic society and his description of druidism widely available to scholars; its publication in English translation in 1604 ensured access to an even greater British readership. By the early decades of the 17th century, all the major texts referring to Druids – Caesar, Tacitus, Pliny, and Ammianus Marcellinus – were in the public domain. The immediate pre-Roman ancestors of the French and British could now be described in all their colourful barbarity, and real personalities with histories could begin to be brought in to enliven the narratives. It is easy to understand how people, tired of unmitigated medieval myths, turned avidly to the new sources. In the warrior Celts, hard-drinking, defiant, and with a love of freedom, they had discovered a worthy ancestor. But the Druids, for all their fascination, were a little more difficult for a Christian intelligentsia to embrace.

Druids as philosophers presented no real difficulty, and it is no surprise that one of the earliest French works on the subject, by Jean Le Fèvre, was entitled *Les Fleurs et Antiquitez des Gaules, où il est traité de Anciens Philosophes Gaulois appellez Druides* (1532). Their judicial role was also emphasized, as in François Meinhard's Latin oration 'The Mistletoe of the Druids as a Symbol of Jurisprudence' (1615). But there was no escaping the descriptions of human sacrifice and the fact that Druids were pagans. When Aylett Sammes came to write *Britannia Antiqua Illustrata* (1676), he rather relished the more gory details, choosing to include an image of a wicker man stuffed with writhing humans and about to be set on fire. John Aubrey, writing of the prehistoric inhabitants of Wiltshire in 1659, has no illusions about the past: he describes the 'shady dismal wood' and 'the inhabitants almost as savage as the beasts whose skins are their only raiment'. This accords well with the views of his contemporary – another Wiltshire resident – the philosopher Thomas Hobbes, who, in 1651, wrote that the life of primitive man was 'solitary, poor, nasty, brutish and short'.

Yet to be acceptable as ancestors, the barbarism had somehow to be mitigated. One way to do this was to present the Celtic past in relation to the anthropological present. The 16th century was a time when lands beyond Europe were beginning to be explored. Magellan's voyage around the world, 1519–22, had brought to notice a bewildering array of 'savage' people, while Raleigh's expedition to the east coast of America in 1585 focused attention on the Virginian Indians, made the more vivid to European audiences by John White's superb depictions of the natives and their daily life. Here were 'noble savages' living in a 'Golden Age'. Jean-Jacques Rousseau, who was later to reflect on these matters in *Social Contract* (1762), saw this as the natural state of mankind but one which could be perverted by the creation of unnatural laws such as those protecting private property and supporting monogamy. The Celts, then, were people living in a simpler state of existence. Their lifestyle was to be admired, but with a tolerance born of hindsight. They were simple and guileless – men who were 'not of evil character', as Strabo had said – and yet ignorance of the Christian god had let their misplaced exuberance for human sacrifice get the better of them. However, the stern Romans had soon persuaded them to turn from their evil ways. Wrapped in this warm patronizing glow, the Celts and their Druids could be made into acceptable forebears.

Yet there were some who were prepared to go further. Concerned by the many interpretations of Christianity that were appearing in the 17th and 18th centuries, and inspired by the laws of nature that scientists were busy discovering, some thinkers, who became known as Deists, put forward the view that there was only one

The Wicker Image.

Government of the BRITAINS.

W. D. fc.

10. Julius Caesar's famous description of humans being sacrificed by being burned in a wicker framework inspired Aylett Sammes's famous image, published in 1676, which has excited the public imagination ever since

Natural Religion though many variant interpretations. While the Deists were regarded by most churchmen as dangerous free-thinkers to be opposed at all cost, some were prepared to try to bring the confusing questions they had raised into some kind of cohesive narrative. One such was the Reverend Henry Rowlands, vicar of Anglesey, who published *Mona Antiqua Restaurata* in 1723. Rowlands argued that since the Britons were descended from Gomer, the grandson of Noah, and the Druids were their priests, the Druids must be the direct inheritors of the religion of Abraham. In the Old Testament Jehovah had called for human sacrifice: in this context, the behaviour of the Druids was entirely understandable. In other words, druidism and Christianity were two closely related branches of the same Patriarchal Religion. This view was taken up enthusiastically by William Stukeley, who saw no inconsistency in embracing druidism and Christianity in his wide ecumenical arms. As we will see, his interpretations of Avebury and Stonehenge, when eventually he came to publish them, were heavily bound up in his belief in a unified Patriarchal Religion.

The medieval chroniclers had taken little notice of the archaeological monuments visible in the countryside, but from the 16th century antiquarians were beginning to develop an interest in the physical remains of the past and to see them as a potential source of evidence. One of the pioneers was John Leland (1503–52), librarian, chaplain, and antiquary to King Henry VIII, who set out on a series of journeys through the English countryside between 1536 and 1542. He died before he could publish his observations, but his copious notes were preserved in the Bodleian Library in Oxford, where they were widely consulted and were eventually published as the *Itinerary of John Leland* by Thomas Hearne between 1710 and 1712. Leland's dogged determination to seek out antiquities and to record them as primary evidence set standards for others. On one of his trips, Leland visited Stonehenge but had little to say other than to repeat the folk tale, recorded by Geoffrey of Monmouth, that the stones had been brought from

Ireland by Merlin 'with remarkable ingenuity and using clever inventions'. Other itinerant antiquarians followed. Inigo Jones (1573–1652) made copious notes and drawings, concluding that the monument was Roman. Others thought it to be Viking, Saxon, or Phoenician, but it was the Wiltshire antiquarian John Aubrey (1626–97) who realized that it must be prehistoric. In 1649, he wrote of the ancient Britons, 'Their religion is at large described by Caesar. Their priests were Druids. Some of their temples I pretend to have restored, as Avebury, Stonehenge etc.' It was from this moment that the link between Stonehenge and other megalithic monuments and Druids passed into the popular imagination, and this has remained a belief adhered to by many even today. Aubrey developed the idea into notes for a book to be called *Templa Druidum* but it was never published. Extracts, however, appeared in the 1695 edition of William Camden's *Britannia* edited by Edmund Gibson.

Aubrey's theory was influential largely, one suspects, because it offered a tangible reality to the increasingly popular theme of Druids. Edward Lhuyd, the Keeper of the Ashmolean Museum at Oxford, who was working on his *Archaeologia*, warmed to the idea, writing of megalithic monuments that '...they were Places of Sacrifice and other religious Rites in the Times of Paganism seeing the Druids were our antient heathen Priests'. Another scholar to embrace Aubrey's views with enthusiasm was John Toland (1670–1722), whose ideas were first published in a series of letters to his patron Lord Molesworth in 1726 and were given wider circulation in a book, *Critical History of the Celtic Religion* (1740), later to appear under the more appealing title of *The History of the Druids*. Toland's contribution to the debate was to integrate the Irish sources which he evidently knew well, but as a dangerous free-thinker his work inspired much hostility.

A more persuasive writer was a Lincolnshire doctor and antiquarian, William Stukeley (1687–1765). He first visited Stonehenge and Avebury in 1719, and for the next five years made

John Aubrey

JOHN AUBREY.

11. John Aubrey, the first writer to connect Druids with Stonehenge, in
the late 17th century. From J. Britton, *Memoirs of John Aubrey* (1845)

regular visits carrying out an impressive programme of fieldwork. His work was accurate and objective, and provided the first detailed survey of both monuments and the cultural landscape in which they were set. His intention was to write a book entitled *The History of the Temple of the Ancient Celts*, but other activities intervened and he was ordained in 1729, turning his attentions to currently popular theories of Patriarchal Christianity which were being advanced by his fellow antiquarian, the Reverend Henry Rowlands. Rowlands' antiquarian studies focused on the monuments and history of his native Anglesey and in his book, *Mona Antiqua Restaurata* (1723), he dwelt with some relish on Tacitus' famous description of the druidic altars 'soaked in human blood'. These altars, Rowlands argued, were the megaliths with which the island abounded. Rowlands' views, published at the time that Stukeley was completing his fieldwork at Stonehenge and Avebury, cannot have failed to have had an impact on Stukeley's thinking.

Eventually, in 1740, Stukeley published *Stonehenge, a Temple restor'd to the British Druids* and three years later, *Abury, a Temple of the British Druids, with Some Others, Described*. Building on the earlier work of Aubrey, he had added his own observations of the physical remains, but the volumes, when they appeared, were part of a complex theological debate about the Patriarchal Religion of Abraham and its uninterrupted progression to druidism and Christianity. To suit his ever-more elaborate theories, Stukeley had no problem in moulding his earlier objective observations to make a better fit. What had begun as an antiquarian exercise based on careful topographical observation ended as a fanciful theological tract designed to protect the Church of England against Deist free-thinking. In the process, the Druids had been provided with an architectural context, placed historically within the development of the Church and altogether comfortably domesticated.

12. A Druid as imagined by Aylett Sammes in a publication of 1676

But what did they actually look like? Aylett Sammes offered a
suitable image in his *Britannia Antiqua Illustrata* (1676). His
Druid stands tall, wearing a knee-length tunic and a hooded
cloak. He is bare-footed but dignified by a prodigious beard. He
carries a staff in his right hand, an open book in his left, and has a
flask at his right side. The image fast became an acceptable icon,

The history of the Temples & religion of the Druids.

The history of the religion and temples of the DRVIDS.

13. William Stukeley's vision of a Druid, no doubt influenced by Sammes, is illustrated in his manuscript *The History of the Religion and Temples of the Druids*, now in the Bodleian Library, Oxford

which both Rowlands and Stukeley independently copied in 1725. Rowlands dispensed with the book and added a branch of oak leaves, preferring to give his Druid sandals. Stukeley also favoured sandals, but his Druid, left hand on chest in pensive mood, sports a beard of less eccentric length and stands beneath an oak tree with an oak grove in the background. The vision of the imagined Druid could easily be mistaken for an Old Testament patriarch. It has provided an enduring model for many later would-be Druids to follow.

By the mid-18th century, then, the rediscovered Druid had been positioned carefully within an intellectual context relevant to the time. In both Britain and France, he was an icon of a distant pre-Roman past, easily understood and part of the acceptable pedigree which gave a dignity to the emerging nations. He also offered a *frisson* of danger – a reminder of the delicate balance between wisdom and savagery. Such a dichotomy played well with the intellectual climate of the time. Classical texts had provided an outline script; 17th- and 18th-century imagination had turned it into a morality play.

All the props were now in place – the stone circles, the sacrificial altars, oak groves, and mistletoe. The Druids could perform as philosophers, bards, teachers, and priests, distanced from the toils of everyday life but always prepared to lead their people against imperialist aggressors when needs required.

It was an engaging creation and one that has persisted.

Chapter 8

Romanticism and the rise of nationalism

In the two centuries or so from c. 1550 to 1750, the Celts and the Druids, seen through the eyes of Greek and Roman writers, were discovered, repackaged as players in the long march of the true Patriarchal Religion, and provided with a landscape of megaliths within which to enact their engaging rituals. To make them even more real to their growing band of admirers, they were visualized as venerable old men, gentle in their rural simplicity. It was an image totally appropriate to the age that created it. And yet it failed, completely, to satisfy. What was missing was the thread of continuity which linked the past to the present: nor was there a literary texture in which to embed the now-familiar image. Not to be outdone, the Romantics of the late 18th century used their hyperactive imaginations to fill these uncomfortable gaps.

Celtomania was now in the air. The Breton priest Paul-Yves Pezron had published his highly influential *L'Antiquité de la Nation et la Langue des Celts* in 1703, and this was followed by the first volume of Edward Lhuyd's *Archaeologia Britannica* in 1707. The two books introduced to the French and the British the attractive concept that they were the direct descendants of the prehistoric Celts and that Celtic cultures survived in the remoter parts of the west – in Brittany, Cornwall, Wales, the Isle of Man, Scotland, and Ireland – where the different dialects of the ancient Celtic language were still spoken in everyday life. Here, then, were the regions where a Celtic literary tradition could be expected to survive and where, just perhaps, some remnant of druidism might have lingered on.

From these early beginnings, enthusiasm for the 'Celtic heritage' grew to become wildly popular. By the late 18th century, Celtic literature was being 'discovered', or invented, while by the end of the 19th century, the 'Celtic personality' had become a worthy subject for lively debate. Celtomania continues today, though usually in a highly commercialized guise redolent of the times.

In France, in particular, the passion for things Celtic grew unabated, fed by a succession of books like Simon Pelloutier's *Histoire des Celtes* (1740), La Tour-d'Auvergn's *Origines Gauloises* (1796), and Jacques Cambray's *Monuments Celtiques* (1805). All dealt enthusiastically with Druids, Cambray introducing the idea that the megalithic monuments of Carnac were related to the practice of druidic astronomy. In Britain, this was the period when scholarly activity began to focus on the production of county histories, in the early chapters of which Celts and Druids featured large.

Reviewing the phenomenon of Celtomania at the beginning of the 20th century, the French archaeologist Salomon Reinach (1858–1932) characterized, with barely hidden irony, the whole exuberant episode:

> The Celts are the oldest people in the world; their language is preserved practically intact in Bas-Breton; they were profound philosophers whose inspired doctrines have been handed down by the Welsh Bardic Schools, dolmens are their altars where their priests the Druids offered human sacrifice; stone alignments were their astronomical observatories.

In this wild enthusiasm for everything 'Celtic', lively imagination continued to transform the concept of the Druid. To understand

what was happening, it is best to consider the Celtic regions
separately.

In England, one of the most creative imaginations to become
enthused with the Druids was the poet William Blake (1757–1827).
In his *Prophetic Books*, written between 1797 and 1804, he
developed the idea that the Holy Land was in fact Britain, and
Jerusalem was located not far from Primrose Hill in London.
It was in Britain that Patriarchal Religion began, and thus 'All
Things Begin and End in Albion's Ancient Druid Rocky Shore'.
Whether he actually believed his own mystic ramblings it is
difficult to say: he was at least prepared to admit that his work
was 'Visionary or Imaginative'.

Other poets revelled in druidic themes. A Scottish minister, the
Reverend John Ogilvie, indulged himself in a poem of dubious
quality, *The Fane of the Druids*, in which a chief Druid, attended
by virgins, officiates beneath an oak tree set in a stone circle
(a *fane*). Here is the archetypal image:

> Though time with silver locks adorn'd his head
> Erect his gesture yet, and firm his tread...
> His seemly beard, to grace his form bestow'd
> Descending decent, on his bosom flow'd;
> His robe of purest white, though rudely join'd
> Yet showed an emblem of the purest mind.

The Druids were now so much a part of English folk culture that
the desire to own a Druid temple caught the imagination of the
elite. Field Marshal Henry Seymour Conway, on his retirement
as Governor of Jersey, was given a megalithic structure by the
grateful islanders. This he transported to his Berkshire home
and in 1788 set it up as a Druid circle at the appropriately named
Temple Combe, where it is still extant. Others, not lucky enough
to have a genuine megalith with which to amuse themselves,
constructed monuments from local materials. A replica of

Stonehenge was built by William Danby (1752–1833) at Swinton Hall, Ilton, Yorkshire, while the Bishop of Bath and Wells, George Henry Law, constructed a roofed structure, somewhat in Gothic mode, at Banwell in about 1820, as a place where he could contemplate the triumph of Christianity over paganism encouraged by the engraved verse:

> Here where once Druids trod in times of yore
> And stain'd their altars with a victim's gore
> Here now the Christian ransomed from above
> Adores a God of mercy and of love.

A desire for more active involvement encouraged others to invent druidical societies. One of the earliest was, appropriately, the Druidical Society of Anglesey, which was set up in 1772 under the authority of an archdruid. It was essentially a charitable organization whose members distinguished themselves by wearing smart blue uniforms enlivened by buttons embossed with Druids' heads. In 1781, another organization, the Ancient Order of Druids, was inaugurated in London. It functioned largely as a Friendly Society for the benefit of its members and after a fission in 1839 it continued (and still continues) to survive.

In England, where successive waves of invaders had broken the thread of continuity with the Celtic past, there was little recourse but to invent things anew, but in the more remote parts of the north and west enthusiasts could seek for direct living links with distant ancestors.

In Wales, they found a bardic tradition still just alive. From at least as early as the 12th century, poets and musicians serving the elite were organized through a court authority whose function it was to maintain standards by means of periodic competitions known as *eisteddfodau*. The *eisteddfod* provided an occasion for the largely migrant performers to gather in one place to hear each other, to compete, and to be awarded licences to perform by the presiding court. By the 16th century, poets and bards were fast disappearing from the households of the Anglicized Welsh aristocracy but still the tradition of the *eisteddfod* was kept up, if only in a haphazard manner.

In 1568, Queen Elizabeth I used the occasion of an *eisteddfod* held in Flintshire as a way to control the increasing number of vagrants now roaming the countryside. To distinguish the genuine performers, her decree encouraged them to attend so that 'all and every Person or Persons that intend to maintain their living by name or Colour of Minstrels, Rythmers or Bards...shall...shew their learning thereby'. Thereafter the fortunes of the *eisteddfod* fluctuated. In 1620, a meeting held in Glamorgan attracted only four people, but in the 18th century growing interest in the Celts began to boost attendances. Further support came in the 1780s, when two recently formed London societies for Welsh expatriates, the Cymmrodorion and the Gwyneddigion, began to offer literary prizes.

One of the members of the Gwyneddigion was Edward Wilson, a London stonemason who preferred to be known by his bardic name Iolo Morganwg. In 1790, he attended the *eisteddfod* held at St Asaph as one of the participating bards, convincing himself that the bards were descended from the Druids and that the *eisteddfod* was in essence a druidic ceremony. Not content with the symbolism of the event, he decided to invent what he considered to be more appropriate rituals. The story is taken up by the *Gentleman's Magazine* of 1792, reporting on a gathering that had taken place on 23 September:

> This being the day on which the autumnal equinox occurred, some Welsh Bards, resident in London, assembled in congress on Primrose Hill, according to ancient usage...The wonted ceremonies were observed. A circle of stones formed, in the middle of which was the *Maen Gorsedd* or altar, on which a naked sword being placed, all the Bards assisted to sheath it.

The entire procedure was concocted in Iolo's hyperactive imagination.

It is quite likely that the nonsenses indulged in on Primrose Hill would have died out had it not been for the opportunity Iolo took to implant his Gorsedd confection onto the unsuspecting *eisteddfod* held at Carmarthen in 1819. The Bishop of St David's, who was presiding, was evidently embarrassed and 'wished the Bard to dispense with some of the initiatory forms', but Iolo triumphed by sheer force of personality. The venerable tradition of the *eisteddfod* has been saddled with Iolo's druidic fabrications ever since.

Iolo claimed that the ancient bardic tradition had survived in his native Glamorganshire unbroken from the time of the Druids and that he had discovered texts and poems to prove this. Moreover, he also claimed to have been admitted a bard 'in the Ancient manner: a custom still retained in Glamorgan but, I believe, in no other part of Wales'. The texts and poems seem to have been another figment of his imagination.

It may have been that Iolo was basing some of his assertions on a series of poems collected by the Reverend Evan Evans and published in a popular book, *Specimens of the Poetry of the Ancient Welsh Bards* (1746). Some of the poems, Evans argued, could be ascribed to a 6th-century poet, Taliesin, and contained the secret lore of the Druids, though he admitted to the obscurity of the texts and the difficulty of translating them. Iolo seized on this work, claiming, in his *Poems, Lyric and Pastoral* (1794), that the poems of Taliesin contained a complete system of druidism and that this was supported by a 16th-century manuscript which presented 20 'Druidic Ordonnances'. The document, like so much of Iolo's 'evidence', simply did not exist. Thus the work of serious scholars like Evans, who set out to collect genuine works of traditional literature, was diminished by attempts to interpret their findings within the Romantic parameters indulged in at the time. Worse were the imaginings and inventions of Iolo, whose self-fulfilling forgeries perverted scholarship for generations to come. In the genuine remnants of the bardic tradition surviving in Wales in the 18th century there is nothing to offer a link to a druidic past.

Celts and Druids continued to dominate Welsh literary studies well into the 19th century, with books like Edward Davies's *Celtic Researches* (1804) and *The Mythology and Rites of the British Druids* (1809), both heavily influenced by the fictions of Iolo. The publication of collections of Welsh stories, first written down in the 11th or 12th centuries, under the title of the *Mabinogi*, by Lady Charlotte Guest (1838, 1840, 1849), added little to the debate. But the foundation of the Cambrian Society in 1845 offered a new start. Welsh scholarship could now look ahead to the time when the realities of archaeological evidence could begin to create a new narrative replacing the fanciful speculations of the past. Yet at the annual ceremony of the *eisteddfod*, the ghost of Iolo must be smiling contentedly to see his spurious inventions dignified by tradition.

The Scots were not to be left out of the rush to discover a Celtic tradition alive and well in the ballads and stories told in the Scottish countryside. In 1760, their hopes were rewarded with the publication of *Fragments of Ancient Poetry Collected in the Highlands of Scotland and Translated from the Gaelic or Erse Language*, compiled by an enthusiastic Scot, James Macpherson (1736–96). The book was an immediate success. The public appetite was insatiable, and Macpherson responded with two more offerings, *Fingal* in 1762 and *Temora* in 1763, based, he claimed, on two 5th-century manuscripts written by a Gaelic bard called Ossian. Needless to say, the manuscripts were never produced and were no doubt a fiction. The best that can be said is that Macpherson may have come across some documents of the 16th century and used these, together with other poetic fragments, to create a saga worthy of national aspirations. 'Ossian', as it became known, was an instant success throughout Europe and was used as an example of the free Celtic spirit to inspire the various freedom movements which were stirring in the early decades of the 19th century. But not all approved of it. Horace Walpole thought it boring; Walter Scott was more outspoken, describing it as 'an absolute tissue of forgeries...absolutely drivelling'. Nowadays Macpherson is seen as a man of his time – an enthusiast whose creative energies completely overshadowed his academic integrity. In a later book, *History of Great Britain*, published in 1773, the Druids inevitably featured large within the context of his earlier imaginative fiction.

Macpherson was creating his vision of a rich Celtic tradition for his native Highlanders at a time of dramatic social and economic change, when, following the suppression of the Jacobite rebellion of 1745, the clan system was being disbanded, setting in train the Highland Clearances and mass movements of population from the land. A desire to find deep roots is an understandable response to social turmoil.

In Brittany, too, society was facing far-reaching changes. The remote Armorican peninsula, linked by the ocean to other regions of Atlantic Europe, had always differed in culture and outlook from the rest of France. From the viewpoint of Paris, it was backward, deeply religious, and in many parts strongly royalist. When the Revolution came in the 1790s, the Bretons rose up against it, inspired both by their abhorrence of the Jacobin 'cult of reason' which threatened their religion, and by their rejection of the centralizing power of Paris, which they saw as a challenge to their cultural identity. The open rebellion of the Breton insurgency – the *Chouans* – against the Revolutionary forces ensured that the country was severely treated – they were, in the eyes of the centre, counter-revolutionary barbarians.

With the restoration of the Bourbons, following the defeat of Napoleon, French society looked afresh at Brittany and saw something quite different. Here were noble savages – Celts – with roots going back deep into time, living in a landscape of monuments inherited from their prehistoric past and steeped in a culture redolent of their Celticity. If the monuments of Carnac were druidic temples, then the living Bretons were their direct descendants and their language, customs, and curious dress were precious survivals from the time when the Druids walked the land. As one writer said of Brittany in 1845: 'It is there that the descendants of the Celts have maintained a dress and a physiognomy which are but druidism in disguise.'

In this new atmosphere of intellectual excitement, a young Breton aristocrat, Vicomte Hersart de La Villemarqué (1815–95), began roaming the countryside collecting ballads and poems which he edited and in 1838 published as *Barzaz-Breiz (Songs of Brittany)* – a book which was immediately proclaimed to be a revelation of the Celtic spirit of Brittany. It set a trend for other collectors who by the end of the century had amassed a huge archive of Breton folklore and traditions.

La Villemarqué was an enthusiastic Celtophile, and in 1838 visited Wales to attend the *eisteddfod* in Abergavenny where he was admitted as a bard. Brimming with excitement, he wrote home to his father: 'I am a bard now, truly a bard! a "titled bard!" and I have been received according to the ancient rituals of the 5th and 6th centuries, handed down to our time.' He made use of his trip to Britain to visit Oxford to consult Welsh manuscripts, and he naturally could not resist a trip to Stonehenge which, at the time, was still regarded to be a Druid temple.

In 1867, La Villemarqué was instrumental in setting up the first Interceltic Congress held at Saint-Brieuc on the northern coast of Brittany and attended by delegates from all the Celtic-speaking countries. By now, some 30 years after the publication of *Barzaz-Breiz*, much more was known of traditional ballads of Brittany and some commentators were beginning to question the authenticity of La Villemarqué's work. Matters came to a head with a devastating critique published by R. F. Le Men to coincide with the Congress in which he taunted, 'Play the bard, play the arch-bard or even the Druid, but do not attempt to falsify history with your inventions.' It looked rather as though La Villemarqué had followed in the footsteps of Iolo Morganwg and James Macpherson by inventing what he had hoped to find. There matters rested for nearly a hundred years until, in the 1960s, his original notebooks were found showing just how much he had been able to glean from the peasants he had interviewed in the 1830s. The doubts expressed by his critics probably arose because by the time a second generation of collectors had taken to the field, many of the old ballad singers had died and their songs with them. The discovery of the notebooks has gone some way to reinstate La Villemarqué's reputation.

With the coming of the railway to Brittany, this once remote corner of France – sought out by those wishing to immerse themselves in *'la vie sauvage'* – became easily accessible to tourists from Paris and visitors from Britain alike who were delighted to find aged storytellers still at work in the tradition of the bards and young women dancing round menhirs in thinly disguised fertility rituals. They could even buy a postcard of the 'Archdruid of Ménez-Hom' – a crabbed old man complete with sickle standing on a megalithic tomb, eyeing an innocent young girl who sits meekly nearby – the Druid-as-wished-for to titillate the tourist!

In Ireland, the rediscovery of the Celtic past took a different trajectory, not least because of the decimation of the population caused by the famine of the 1840s which destroyed much of the rich traditional culture of the island. In 1852, the antiquarian Sir William Wilde wrote: 'The old forms and customs…are becoming obliterated; the festivals are unobserved and the rustic festivities neglected or forgotten.' Yet 50 years later, Lady Gregory was surprised by the splendour of the traditional tales told to her by the poor of Galway which she recorded in her *Poets and Dreamers* (1903). The year before she had produced her free translation of the stories of the Ulster Cycle in *Cuchulain of Muirthemne,*

2289. – L'Archi-Druide du Ménez-Hom

14. 'The Archdruid of Ménez-Hom'. A postcard of the early 20th century, popular among tourists to Brittany, perpetuating the belief that druidism survived into recent Breton folk culture

15. The tradition of the storyteller, as here depicted in Emile Eugène Fauconnier's painting of 1908, continued well into the 20th century in Brittany. Some would see this as the last genuine link with a past in which a skilled group communicated oral traditions

bringing to a wide audience the epic of the *Táin* with its echoes of a lost Celtic world peopled by heroes and by Druids like the manipulative Cathbad and Finnegas the Bard.

Stories of Celtic heroes fighting for their freedoms flowing into romantic visions of the mystical Celt 'capable of profound feelings, and of an adorable delicacy in his religious instincts' (Ernest Renan), provided inspiration for those fighting for the survival of their traditional cultures in Brittany, Wales, Ireland, and Scotland. The 'Celtic spirit' stood in defiance of the centralizing imperatives of London and Paris – but the Druid was hardly to be seen. He was now relegated to the shadows, a relic of a past no longer acceptable in the creation of national identities.

Chapter 9
Neodruids and the neopagans

The creation of neodruidic societies, beginning with the formation of the Druidic Society of Anglesey in 1772 and the Ancient Order of Druids in 1781, was, as we have seen, rooted in late 18th-century Romanticism. This was the time of a nation-wide vogue for societies of all kinds – societies serving new-found needs for people to come together with like-minded fellows in gatherings focused on mutual interests, offering the reassurance of group identity at a time when rapid social and economic change was disrupting and destroying traditional values. Societies took many forms. One of the more common were the charitable institutions set up for the benefit of members and their families, often with a wider brief to help society at large. These were the Benefit and Friendly societies inspired by the ideals of Freemasonry. Many adopted a distinct theme around which to organize their beliefs and ceremonies and it was only to be expected, in the age of Romantic Celtomania, that druidism would commend itself as an identifier – thus, the Druidic Society of Anglesey and the Ancient Order of Druids.

The Druidic Society of Anglesey included among its membership most of the local clergy and landowners. They contributed an average of 34 guineas annually to a fund used for a variety of good causes – most notably supporting apprenticeships for poor children and funding local agricultural societies by offering prizes for agricultural innovation. Grants were also given to support hospitals in Chester and Liverpool, as well as to help the poor and needy. The trappings of druidism were kept to a minimum, though harpists were employed to enliven the meetings. When eventually the society was wound up in 1884, the remaining funds were divided between hospitals and supporting rescue at sea.

The Ancient Order of Druids was set up by a London carpenter and builder, Henry Hurle, in the Kings Arms tavern in Oxford Street as a simple Benefit Society, but it soon grew in popularity taking on the structure of Freemasonry instituted in the early decades of the century. In its early years, the Ancient Order of Druids was essentially a social club for prosperous working people who came together for entertainment—listening to music and singing, reading poetry and attending talks on scientific and artistic themes; they also supported charitable aims. As its popularity grew, Lodges were set up in other parts of the country and abroad, and by 1831 total membership numbered over 200,000 spread over 193 Lodges, with some as far afield as America, Canada, and India.

With the growth came greater constitutional complexity which coincided with the changing needs of members, particularly those in the industrial areas of the Midlands and the North. Tensions emerged which led to dissent and division. The principal issue of contention was the desire of many of the Lodges in industrial regions to adopt the structures of a Benefit Society so that funds could be more easily used to support members in need. This was resisted by the wealthy Grand Lodge. Matters came to a head in December 1833, when the movement split, the Grand Lodge and its supporters retaining the original title while the rebels re-formed under the title of the 'United Ancient Order of Druids'.

The subsequent history of both Orders was dominated by fission and secession, too tedious to recount. The only linking factor between them was the retention of the word 'Druid' in the title. One of the scions, the United Ancient Order of Female Druids, founded in 1876, reflects the growing recognition of women in Victorian society.

Whilst these 'druidic' organizations usually enlivened their proceedings with the trappings of romantic druidism – white robes, false beards, mistletoe, oak leaves, and the like – and used terms like 'Archdruid' and 'First Bard', some making quite spurious claims to legitimate descent from the Druids of the Classical world, they were, in essence, Benefit Societies and Freemasonry organizations serving the real social, economic, and emotional needs of a significant sector of the population caught up in the exponential changes spanning the period from the late 18th century to the early decades of the 20th century.

With the development of the Welfare State in the post-Second World War period, the need for such organizations greatly diminished, and the trappings and rituals of these old societies, still steeped in the fustiness of the Victorian era, became increasingly irrelevant to the post-war generation. Gradually the factions have died away through inertia or fission to the point of extinction. One of the last to go, towards the end of the 1990s, was the United Ancient Order of Druids, leaving the original parent, the Ancient Order of Druids, as the last survivor of its many offspring. One reason for its longevity probably lies in its 'aristocratic' tradition. Before the schism of 1833, the Ancient Order had adopted a hierarchical structure which allowed an elite to distinguish itself from the general membership. This made it more attractive to the upper classes who could meet among their peers. Perhaps the most famous occasion, in the public domain, was the meeting of the Oxford-based Albion Lodge of the Ancient Order on 15 August 1908 in the grounds of Blenheim Palace at the invitation of the Duke of Marlborough, who was himself a member. It was at that meeting that the young Winston Churchill, recently appointed as President of the Board of Trade, was initiated into the Ancient Order. A photograph of the occasion shows the young man, in a tightly buttoned suit with wing

16. A meeting of the Ancient Order of Druids held at Blenheim, Oxfordshire, on 15 August 1908, at which Winston Churchill was introduced into the Order

collar, surrounded by sickle-carrying Druids looking decidedly uncomfortable in ill-fitting white robes and hoods and ungainly long white beards. In later life, as a serious historian, one suspects he might have regretted the photograph, if not the occasion.

If the post-war period saw the virtual demise of the fraternal Druids, it was by no means the time of the decline of neodruidism. The 1960s, with its sense of new freedoms and new values tinged with an eagerness to explore mysticism, proved to be fertile ground for what has come to be a rapid growth in the invention and practice of neopagan beliefs. More recently, as the 'green' movement has gathered strength, so neopaganism has increased in its popularity.

Neopaganism takes many forms, with Shamanism, Odinism, Wicca, and Neodruidism being among the more prominent. All share a reverence for the natural world and a sense of being one with it, and all respect the rhythm of the seasons, many choosing to hold their ceremonies on the solstices or at the time of the four major ceremonies of the Celtic calendar. There is also a widespread belief in the polarity of the deity – the competing but balanced opposites of the male and female components. In professing these values, the neopagans have gone back to some of the essential elements that can be discerned in the belief systems of pre-Roman Celtic Europe and, in particular, of Ireland. This has been a conscious seeking-out and selection of those values and beliefs that satisfy current needs. With growing concerns about the future of the planet, it is likely that this form of paganism will attract increasing numbers of followers.

Within this broad neopagan context, a number of groups styling themselves Druids have emerged. One of the largest and more successful of these is the Order of Bards, Ovates and Druids which was founded in 1964. Its principal aims are to help the individual develop his/her innate capacities to the full and to respect and care for the natural world. Its well-organized website (http://www.druidry.org) begins with the all-embracing statement:

> Druidry has become a vital and dynamic Nature-based spirituality that is flourishing all over the world, and that unites our love of the Earth with our love of creativity and the Arts. And flowing through all the exciting new developments in modern Druidism is the power of an ancient tradition: the love of land, sea and sky – the love of the Earth our home.

The Order runs a correspondence course enabling members to aspire to the grades of Bards, Ovates and Druids (the first course is currently available also in an audiovisual version). Another group, the Insular Order of Druids, founded in 1993, recognizes the same three grades, basing their understanding of the attributes and functions of each closely upon those defined in the Posidonian tradition; thus the Bard is the storyteller and the singer of ballads; the Ovate practises divination and is proficient in philosophy; while the Druid helps initiates to harmonize with the natural world.

Druidic groups are proliferating worldwide and take on many different forms to cater for the particular needs of their memberships. The old Ancient Order of Druids still retains the predominantly male orientation of its Masonic tradition, but most of the more recent groups are open equally to both sexes. In America, the Golden Gate Group of San Francisco caters for gay and lesbian Druids who worship at a stone circle dedicated to members who have died from AIDS. Another specialist order are the Hassidic Druids, who combine aspects of Hebrew tradition with Druidic beliefs.

The followers of druidism have responded creatively to the hippy counter-culture of the 1960s and the growing interest in green politics and the environment: their modified style of druidism, in harmony with nature, sits comfortably with the broader concerns

17. One of the many groups of modern Druids, meeting at Stonehenge in 1983

of an increasing sector of the world's population. But some groups are now moving into more controversial areas by claiming rights over prehistoric burials unearthed in archaeological excavations: this is bringing them into direct conflict with the scientific community. How this phase in the evolution of druidism eventually plays out it will be interesting to see: it would be a pity if what is now a gentle and broadly sympathetic package of beliefs and practices were to take on the hectoring and aggressive mode of many of today's other belief systems.

Chapter 10
So, who were the Druids?

Implicit in the title of this chapter is the belief that the Druids were a phenomenon of the past and that those who, since the 17th century, have called themselves Druids cannot claim any degree of continuity with ancient druidic practice.

The evidence we have explored shows that the elite class of 'the wise' – Bards, Vates, and Druids – was rapidly changing in the early 1st millennium AD, even in Ireland where the impact of the Roman world was slight. Internal changes in the structure of society and the fast-growing influence of Christianity were the prime movers in the demise of druidism: the Viking incursion and the impact of Anglo-Norman settlers completed the process. All that remained in the Celtic fringes of Britain and Ireland were itinerant bards, ballad players, and storytellers roaming the countryside. Even in Brittany, which enjoyed a high degree of separation from France, nothing remained except for a few dishevelled raconteurs beloved of the postcard manufacturers of the pre-Great War era.

The increasing availability of Classical texts in the 16th century and the burning desire of Renaissance man to understand his past led, as we have seen, to a passion for Celtic history and with it a fascination with the Druids. Since then, every generation has recreated Druids in a mode satisfying to the aspirations and emotional needs of the time. The 18th century was a time of fanciful inventions and wild fabrications; the 19th century saw a vision of the Druids giving a risqué glamour to Benefit Societies and Masonic Lodges; while in the late 20th century, neopagans have tried to rediscover some of the basic underlying values of prehistoric religions in an attempt to create a belief system compatible with the concerns and values of the green movement. All these manifestations are an engaging part of post-medieval social history, but they are totally irrelevant to our central question – who were the Druids? It is to this that we must finally return.

There is sufficient evidence to suggest that a religious class, among whom were practitioners called Druids, was in existence in western parts of Europe by the 4th century BC, but it is not until the 2nd and 1st centuries BC that the structure of that class comes more clearly into focus with its broad threefold division of Bards, Vates, and Druids. The Bards served as the poets and songwriters who had powers to enhance or destroy a reputation; the Vates were the diviners able to interpret signs to foretell the future; while the Druids were the philosophers, teachers, and the intermediaries between humanity and the gods. The Classical texts are sufficiently explicit to suggest that by the 1st century BC changes were under way which were hastened by the impact of Romanization.

One of the most interesting questions is wherein lay the origins of druidism? It is no longer acceptable to see it as the religion of a group of Celts emerging in west-central Europe and spreading to the west, south, and east through migratory movements: this is too simplistic an interpretation of a highly complex situation. Moreover, there is a growing consensus that it may have been in the Atlantic zone of Europe that the Celtic language originated. This brings us back to Caesar's assertion that druidism originated in Britain and that those who wished to study it had to go there for the purpose. It is quite likely that Caesar was repeating a generally held belief based on Gaulish tradition. How valid was the tradition we cannot say, but it might reflect a long-held view that the Atlantic zone of Europe lay at the heart of the ancient Celtic world.

Our brief review of ritual beliefs and practices in western Europe suggests that there were many practices, going back to the 4th and 3rd millennia, that might hint at a degree of continuity spanning the prehistoric period. That many of the megalithic monuments and chambered tombs were laid out in respect of alignments related to the solstices implies that by the 3rd millennium societies along the Atlantic seaboard had an intimate knowledge of celestial movements which they respected and incorporated into the physical world in which they lived. Deliberate deposition in the ground and in watery contexts and the digging of deep ritual shafts are traditions that go back deep into time, and in the treatment of the human body after death there are indications which could be thought to reflect a belief that the spirit moves on, a belief Classical writers attributed specifically to the Druids. At a more basic level, the focus on the human head in 1st-century religious ritual can be traced back to the Neolithic period.

On the basis of these links, it could be argued that the belief system that underpins druidism extends back in time to the Neolithic period or, put another way, that druidism, as it is recorded in the late 1st millennium, is simply a manifestation of the religious beliefs and practices that had developed over the previous three millennia in Atlantic Europe. If this scenario were accepted, then it would be legitimate to argue that megalithic monuments, including Stonehenge and Avebury, were the structures of the Druids – a view that would have gladdened the hearts of Aubrey, Stukeley, and the Breton *Celtomanes*.

However, the situation is, as always, more complex. Standing back from the mass of data now available, it is possible to identify a period of quite substantial social and economic change in the development of western European society around the middle of the 2nd millennium BC. It is as though one cycle of development, which began with the introduction of the Neolithic economy, came to an end and another began. The changes are quite significant. The megalithic tradition of monument and tomb building ceased, as did the emphasis on ancestral burial in collective tombs. In its place, burials at first focused on individuals, often interred under round barrows, and the predominant inhumation rite quickly gave way to cremation, with the cremated remains of individuals often placed in urns buried in cemeteries. Broadly parallel with this dramatic shift in belief systems came a socioeconomic change which saw the control of the landscape increase, with the laying out of permanent boundaries and extensive systems of fields, and the establishment of long-lasting settlements, usually defined by prominent enclosing earthworks. It was as though the community had now, at last, imposed itself on the land rather than being subservient to it. It was at this time that storage pits began to be dug into the protective earth, and propitiatory offerings placed in the ground and in watery contexts began to increase greatly in number.

This dramatic systems change does not appear to have happened suddenly but was probably largely completed within the first half of the 2nd millennium BC. What caused it is a matter requiring intricate debate for which there is no time here, but one of the prime movers may well have been an overall increase in population and with it greater mobility.

It is a not unreasonable suggestion that it may have been as part of these mid-2nd-millennium changes that druidism emerged. The heavy dependence of the community on the productivity of the land, and the routines which ensured success, would have required a calendar responsive to seasonal changes rather than one predicated on the solstices. It may have been in this context that time division by lunar month came into prominence – a system manifest in the Coligny calendar and the four seasonal festivals that have survived in Irish tradition. It was probably also at a time of increased reliance on the wellbeing of corn-growing and animal husbandry that propitiatory offerings placed in the earth and in watery contexts became a significant pattern of behaviour emphasizing the dependence of the living community on the chthonic deities. In such a context, the conceptual balance between territory/earth/female and tribal/sky/male could readily have emerged or been enhanced. Thus it is possible to identify a real and direct continuity in belief systems, seen in western Europe at the time of the earliest Roman contact, that go back in time to the middle centuries of the 2nd millennium BC. It is therefore not unreasonable to suggest that druidism, which becomes dimly apparent in the Classical sources in the 4th century BC, may have had its origins in the profound changes taking place a thousand years before. That said, some of the knowledge and skills practised by the Druids may have derived from even further back in time.

The demise of the druidic tradition came fast. Within what became the Roman Empire many of the practices were deliberately repressed and the old religion was made irrelevant by the overlay of Romanized beliefs: native gods were systematically conflated with Roman deities, alien religions were introduced, including a variety of eastern mystery religions, and religious practice was brought to conform to a Roman format. No doubt in the deep countryside and away from heavily urbanized areas, old pagan practices continued, but in the turbulent period of the Germanic migrations and the subsequent resettlement, and with the rise of Christianity that followed, what little remained of the old belief systems disappeared altogether, leaving only a murmur of dimly remembered folklore to echo what had been.

In Ireland, beyond the heavy hand of Romanization, it is possible to see something of the process by which Christianity inexorably replaced druidism. Clergy took over the power of Druids, who became degraded as cheap magicians; the Vates became the clerics – the skilled intelligentsia who supported the edifice of the Church, while the Bards were left to compose their poems and songs to amuse or irritate their masters so long as the old social systems should last. By the 17th century – the Druids long gone – the last remnants of the ancient tradition of an intellectual elite had faded into the landscape.

Further reading

The literature on the Druids and the world that they inhabited is huge, varying from the sober and scholarly to the frankly lunatic. I have offered a series of short lists here, sufficient to introduce the subject, together with a list of the most accessible books dealing specifically with the Druids. I need hardly stress I have avoided books at the lunatic end of the spectrum and those more notable for their illustrations than their texts. All the sources quoted have ample bibliographies.

The European prehistoric background
B. Cunliffe (ed.), *The Oxford Illustrated History of Prehistoric Europe* (Oxford: Oxford University Press, 1994).
B. Cunliffe, *Europe between the Oceans* (London: Yale University Press, 2008).
K. Kristiansen, *Europe before History* (Cambridge: Cambridge University Press, 1998).
K. Kristiansen and T. B. Larsson, *The Rise of Bronze Age Society* (Cambridge: Cambridge University Press, 2005).

The Celts
M. Chapman, *The Celts: The Construction of a Myth* (New York: St Martin's Press, 1992).
J. R. Collis, *The Celts: Origins, Myths and Inventions* (Stroud: Tempus, 2003).
B. Cunliffe, *The Ancient Celts* (Oxford: Oxford University Press, 1997).

B. Cunliffe, *The Celts: A Very Short Introduction* (Oxford: Oxford University Press, 2003).

M. J. Green (ed.), *The Celtic World* (London: Routledge, 1995).

J. Hayward, *The Historical Atlas of the Celtic World* (London: Thames and Hudson, 2001).

S. James, *The Atlantic Celts: Ancient Peoples or Modern Invention?* (London: British Museum Press, 1999).

J. T. Koch, R. Karl, A. Minard, and S. O'Faoláin, *An Atlas for Celtic Studies: Archaeology and Names in Ancient Europe and Early Medieval Ireland, Britain and Brittany* (Oxford: Oxbow, 2007).

S. Moscati (ed.), *The Celts* (Milan: Bompiani, 1991).

H. D. Rankin, *Celts and the Classical World* (London: Croom Helm, 1987).

Classical and insular vernacular literature

M. Dillon, *Early Irish Literature* (Chicago: University Press of Chicago, 1948).

H. J. Jackson, *The Oldest Irish Tradition: A Window on the Iron Age* (Cambridge: Cambridge University Press, 1964).

T. Kinsella (tr.), *The Táin* (Oxford: Oxford University Press, 1969).

J. T. Koch (ed.), *The Celtic Heroic Age* (Malden, MA: Celtic Studies Publications, 1994).

J. J. Tierney, 'The Celtic Ethnography of Posidonius', *Proceedings of the Royal Irish Academy*, Vol. 60 (1960), 189–275.

Celtic religion

J. L. Brunaux, *The Celtic Gauls: Gods, Rites and Sanctuaries* (London: Seaby, 1988).

M. Green, *The Gods of the Celts* (Gloucester: Alan Sutton, 1968).

P. MacCana, *Celtic Mythology* (Feltham: Newnes Books, 1968).

M.-L. Sjoestedt, *Gods and Heroes of the Celts* (Dublin: Four Courts Press, 1994).

The Druids

M. Aldhouse-Green, *Caesar's Druids* (Yale: Yale University Press, 2010).

N. K. Chadwick, *The Druids* (Cardiff: University of Wales Press, 1966).

P. B. Ellis, *A Brief History of the Druids* (London: Constable, 1994).

M. J. Green, *Exploring the World of the Druids* (London: Thames and Hudson, 1968).

Druids

R. Hutton, *The Druids* (London: Hambledon Continuum, 2007).

T. D. Kendrick, *The Druids: A Study in Keltic Prehistory* (London: Methuen, 1927).

A. L. Owens, *The Famous Druids: A Survey of Three Centuries of English Literature* (Oxford: Oxford University Press, 1962).

S. Piggott, *The Druids* (London: Thames and Hudson, 1968).

Index

THE TUDORS
A Very Short Introduction
John Guy

First published as part of the best-selling *Oxford Illustrated History of Britain*, John Guy's Very Short Introduction to the Tudors is the most authoritative short introduction to this exciting long century. It offers a compelling account of the political, religious, and economic changes of the country under such leading monarchs as Henry VIII and Elizabeth I.

This book has been substantially revised and updated for this edition. In particular, the reigns of Henry VII, Edward VI, and Philip and Mary are comprehensively reassessed.

www.oup.co.uk/isbn/0-19-285401-1